HOW
SUCCESSFUL
PEOPLE WIN

Other Hay House Titles by Ben Stein

HOW TO RUIN YOUR LIFE (hardcover)
(also available as an audio book)

HOW TO RUIN YOUR LOVE LIFE

HOW TO RUIN YOUR FINANCIAL LIFE

HOW TO RUIN YOUR LIFE
(tradepaper that comprises the three titles above)

❀ ❀ ❀

Other Titles by Ben Stein and Phil DeMuth
(New Beginnings Press imprint)

CAN AMERICA SURVIVE?:
The Rage of the Left, the Truth, and What to Do about It

YES, YOU CAN BE A SUCCESSFUL INCOME INVESTOR!:
Reaching for Yield in Today's Market

YES, YOU CAN STILL RETIRE COMFORTABLY!:
The Baby-Boom Retirement Crisis and How to Beat It

❀ ❀ ❀

All of the above are available at your
local bookstore, or may be ordered by visiting:

Hay House USA: **www.hayhouse.com**®
Hay House Australia: **www.hayhouse.com.au**
Hay House UK: **www.hayhouse.co.uk**
Hay House South Africa: **orders@psdprom.co.za**
Hay House India: **www.hayhouseindia.co.in**

HOW SUCCESSFUL PEOPLE WIN

Using "Bunkhouse Logic"
to Get What You Want in Life

BEN STEIN

HAY HOUSE, INC.
Carlsbad, California
London • Sydney • Johannesburg
Vancouver • Hong Kong • Mumbai

Published and distributed in the United States by: Hay House, Inc.: www.
hayhouse.com • **Published and distributed in Australia by:** Hay House
Australia Pty. Ltd.: www.hayhouse.com.au • **Published and distributed
in the United Kingdom by:** Hay House UK, Ltd.: www.hayhouse.co.uk •
Published and distributed in the Republic of South Africa by: Hay House SA
(Pty), Ltd.: orders@psdprom.co.za • **Distributed in Canada by:** Raincoast:
www.raincoast.com • **Published in India by:** Hay House Publications (India)
Pvt. Ltd.: www.hayhouseindia.co.in • **Distributed in India by:** Media Star:
booksdivision@mediastar.co.in

Editorial supervision: Jill Kramer   *Design:* Tricia Breidenthal

Originally published as *Bunkhouse Logic* in November 1981 by Avon
Books. ISBN: 0-380-78543-9

Library of Congress Cataloging-in-Publication Data

Stein, Ben.
  How successful people win: using "bunkhouse logic" to get what you
want in life / Ben Stein.
     p. cm.
  ISBN 1-56170-975-1
  1. Success—Psychological aspects. I. Title.
  BF637.S8 S692 2003
  158.1—dc21
                                           2002152081

ISBN 13: 978-1-56170-975-5
ISBN 10: 1-56170-975-1

08 07 06 05 4 3 2 1
1st Hay House printing, September 2005

Printed in the United States of America

CONTENTS

PREFACE

I remember the day I reached the breaking point.

It was August of 1973. On a morning in the middle of the month, in Washington, D.C., I piled into my car and headed for work. By 9 A.M., the temperature was well over 90 degrees, and the humidity was close to 100 percent. My car, a 1972 Subaru, had no air-conditioning. I drove through the elegant residential section of Georgetown, past the new, prestigious office buildings on K Street, and aimed for the low-rent district, where my office was.

On the corner of 11th and Pennsylvania Avenue, *The Washington Star* once had its office. But the *Star,* although on the verge of bankruptcy, had decided that the neighborhood was far too squalid for the general well-being of its employees. It had moved, and left the building to be infested by rats and winos. After a few months, the federal government took over the building, steam-cleaned the walls, put in fiberboard partitions, and started renting the space to the most lowly government agencies. That was where my office was—I was a trial attorney for the Federal Trade Commission.

At about 9:30, I pulled into the garage next to the building. The garage was seven levels deep. By the time I reached the seventh level, the heat and dust were intense. Drunks lurked in the corners, making hideous grunting sounds. I took myself up to the street level and squinted in the sunlight. A few feet away from me were still more derelicts lined up against the wall of the old *Star* building, urinating against the wall. In broad daylight they stood there. No policeman, no building guard, no one at all stopped them. I hurried past them into my building.

But the door to my office was closed. On it was a sign telling me that my office had been assigned to someone else. I was to report to room 710. Obviously, no one had consulted me, and naturally, that was par for the course.

I walked down the linoleum halls with their lime-green fiberboard partitions and managed not to disturb the secretaries who were playing games with their children. You see, in *our* office, the secretaries simply refused to do any work, and their bosses were far too craven to insist that any work be done, so the secretaries brought their families to the office and spent their days playing and listening to the radio.

When I saw my new space, I felt my heart muscles constrict dangerously. Room 710 was a broom closet that should not have been assigned to a janitor on probation. It was so narrow that I couldn't get past the edge of my desk to get behind it without walking sideways. It was so shallow that it didn't have room for a chair in front of the desk.

In a frenzy of anger, I rushed to my boss's office to demand to know why I'd been installed in that insulting, tiny cubicle. But he was in Minnesota. I went to the deputy bosses, two giggling numbskulls whose only visible skills lay in flattering the boss.

"It's just temporary," they said. "You'll be moved soon." They both clipped their nails while they spoke to me.

"When?" I asked.

"We don't know," they said. "Sometime soon."

With that, I was dismissed. I went back to my horrible office, feeling desperate. Through my small window, I could see a haze of bus exhaust rising up from Pennsylvania Avenue toward my cell. It was seven floors down to the pavement. That would do the trick.

A messenger arrived, visibly staggering from the effects of marijuana, and laid a file folder on my desk. It was an assignment from my deputy bosses. Apparently there had been complaints about the Vegematic product, and I was being ordered to buy one to see if it really *could* slice ripe tomatoes. "The results of your investigation should be reported to us no later than one month from now," said the accompanying memorandum.

Without meaning to, I started to cry. Something had gone terribly wrong with my life. I'd gone to good schools, where we'd all been told that we were the cream of the crop of humanity, destined to win its glittering prizes at early ages. The same man (me) who now parked his car in a garage whose air would have shamed a 19th-century coal mine had contemplated the greatest mysteries of social organization at the feet of men who guided the destiny of the world. This same man who had to walk gingerly past urinating bums in a section of town considered unsafe for tourists had been elected by his fellow law students to speak to them at their graduation about the meaning of law and life.

Now, just a few short years after graduating from law school in a sunny haze of expectation and pride, I was sitting in a cubicle on the whim of cretinous jackasses, ordered to determine whether a Vegematic would slice a tomato cleanly, and being gradually overcome by fumes from the street below.

Could I quit? Of course not. I had no money. I was lucky if I could pay my credit-card bill every month. I had enough funds to live for maybe two weeks without a paycheck.

Could I get another job? Perhaps, but the prospects weren't good.

Maybe I could change my name and start again in another city. Then again, there was always that seventh-floor window. . . .

I started to ruminate upon my friends' situations. There was little encouragement. The men and women who'd gone to school, taken the right courses, and done their homework might have more elegant offices, and they might be in better parts of town (although some were in actual combat zones of major cities), but almost all of them knew that they were trapped. Some made more money and some made less, but none of them were making *real* money, the kind that buys the true showpieces of human life.

When we'd get together for dinner, we'd all worry about whether we'd have enough money to leave a good tip. When our American Express bills came in the mail, our hearts went into our mouths. We drove old cars and took chartered-flight vacations even as we headed toward our 30th years on earth.

We found ourselves at the mercy of petty tyrants in the forms of junior partners or deputy assistant directors or secretaries who brought their infant children to the office. Instead of the limitless vistas of opportunity that we assumed were on our horizons, we looked out into eight-by-six-foot offices with lime green walls, and onto steamy downtown streets clogged with exhaust.

Even the most brilliant of us were working on small matters that led nowhere intellectually, financially, or socially.

I stepped back and thought about the people I knew from high school as well as those from college and law school. Their desperation was just as great. Trapped as junior salesmen; as adjusters; as operatives within huge bureaucracies, private or public, they saw the same miserable frustration in their lives as everyone else I knew.

If my life and the lives of my friends yielded cold comfort in terms of work, we were even more barren in terms of personal satisfaction. If we were married (I was divorced), we were *unhappily* married. Man and wife joined together in the hope and trust that their lives would be close facsimiles of the lives of the beautiful people, only with more satisfaction. Picture the lives of Marilyn Monroe and a young Howard Hughes melded together in glamorous fusion, and that was what we thought our lives would be.

Instead, we all stared at the ceiling trying to imagine how we might possibly pay our debts to our hopes. We lived in small, drab apartments along with the other uninspired failures of the world. We went to parties where Gallo was served in plastic cups. We thought we might be the inheritors of the fine trophies of life, but instead, we found ourselves mired in frustration at seeing those trophies recede day by day. Like all human beings, we took out that frustration on our spouses. In desperate furtive affairs, we tried to convince ourselves that there was some merit in us, something worthy of redemption if only through the flesh. Of course, it never worked.

Once you're trapped in the cell of the Humiliation Penitentiary, one or two conjugal visits or even *extra* conjugal visits do not set you free.

If we weren't married, our lives were alternately filled and emptied via desperate gropings with partners just as forlorn and angry as we were. We dated within our set—the huge mass of men and women who'd done what we were told, only to have incontrovertible evidence of life's futility thrown in our faces. We were a miserable group. We could hardly bring comfort to one another, as we experienced none of it ourselves. Far from being "swinging singles," we were "brooding singles" or "moping singles."

So there I was on that August day in room 710 of the old *Star* building, wishing I were dead. And there were millions, tens of millions, of others in my exact situation—trapped without hope, without joy, trembling in the certain knowledge of our failure.

Of course, I had to acknowledge that there *were* men and women in the world who were happy. These were the precious few who were getting just the opportunities and pleasures out of life that they wanted. While we stood in line at the Burger King of life, some people were royally waited upon and served at the "21" Club of life's possibilities. At the same moments that we measured our unhappiness in tanker truckloads, others calculated their present and future accomplishments by the supertanker.

I saw them in the offices of the powerful and the rich and the fulfilled. I was the beggar with his face pressed up against the glass window, while the diners inside made merry. When I passed by the White House or by an elegant office emptying of cheerful, bustling men and women, I felt a tangible longing, as if I'd been separated from my birthright. I looked in glossy magazines and saw the pretty people frolicking in Malibu, raking in money and creative fulfillment. On the television news, I watched the movers and shakers press forward in their conquest of life's goodies. I sank further and further into oblivion.

It hurt. In fact, on that August day in 1973, it hurt so much that I couldn't take it any longer. I was a prisoner on death row who had nothing to lose by trying to break out.

I was determined to tear up the road map that had been given to me and start to find new bearings. I knew that the whole program I'd followed and that had been charted for me for the rest of my life could and must be thrown into the trash heap. I promised myself that I would either discover the route to fulfillment or die trying. No amount of effort, no amount of humiliation in the attempt, could be more punishing than what I was going through each and every day. I had to get off the floor and start achieving something worthwhile.

※ ※ ※

Since that time, I've studied the ways of the successful virtually every waking moment—and some sleeping ones, too. Through persistence, I elevated myself into arenas where the successful played and challenged one another. At the White House, I encountered accomplished, confident people who believed that the world was their oyster. I watched their habits and methods. I asked them questions about how they'd moved from square one to the positions of influence and optimism they now held. *Why*, I asked myself, *were these people—objectively no smarter than my friends or I—so far ahead on the one-way street of life? What habits and attitudes did the successful cultivate that put them above ground, triumphing every day, while the mass of others and I sweltered in our dark and airless underground failure chambers? How did the power players see the world? What tricks, conscious or unconscious, did they use to get traction in the world while we others slipped in the mud?*

Not surprisingly, I discovered that the lives of the cabinet secretaries, the movers and shakers of the press, and the captains of industry who had gone into government service were indeed different from my life, and from the way that life had been preached to me. The distinctions were at first nebulous and blurry, but before long, they became sharper. Those high achievers were on a different railroad line altogether. Those girls and boys who found happiness in their work and in their homes were definitely operating off a set of instructions unlike the ones that had been issued to the rest of us. On the coldest of psychic mornings, when our engines would barely turn over, their motors would always start on the first try.

I also took note of why the failures failed. During that particular White House era—the Nixon White House—there was a perfectly adequate sample of self-destructive, self-sabotaging behavior, as well as successful, self-promoting behavior. And I began to see clearly that the failures were on the same guidance system I'd been on.

When I was rather certain that I could differentiate between the useful and the useless attitudes—those that led up and those that led nowhere—I took the first hesitant, tentative steps toward actually behaving in the ways that seemed to lead somewhere promising.

What a shock! I imitated the behavior of the successful, and it carried me toward success. It was like watching a rodeo performance of bull riding for a year, studying every detail of how the cowboy stayed on the bull, and then climbing aboard the bull and staying on myself. The feeling was exhilarating. The thought suddenly struck me that I wasn't necessarily destined to be a failure after all. That thought was heavenly.

Later, from the ashes of that same Nixon White House, I regarded the world at large. A moment of decision: Should I take a chance on the new techniques and try to get a decent job, or use the old time-honored methods, which would lead to a secure failure? What a question.

Like a man practicing a swan dive for the first time, I nervously prepared to go for the good things in life, to take the new path. I flung myself off the board, pretending that I knew how it was done. It worked.

Other people believed that I was a successful man. Job offers poured in. There was no chance at all that I would have to return to the old *Star* building. I had seen the way to fly, and I was flying.

I worked for a time at *The Wall Street Journal,* where I wrote columns and editorials—about popular culture primarily—but also about politics and economics. I had the chance to see successful men and women in action in many areas. I watched and took note of the billionaire investment bankers. I scrutinized the adored writers and publishers. I examined the senators who knew how to get their agendas through Congress.

As I'd done at the White House, I took careful mental notes on how the successful behaved, discerning what set them apart from the unsuccessful. Just as it was at the White House, there were certain behavior and attitude patterns that were the province of the accomplished. The successful were different from you and me. There was absolutely no doubt about it. The men and women who were destined to be happy and prosperous in every way knew some things that most other people never figured out. They were endowed with the habits of success instead of failure.

In many cases, these habits and attitudes were almost instinctual. They had either been picked up at home, or in such a haphazard way that the successful, had they been asked to explain how they did it, would have had a very difficult time. But by the same token, Babe Ruth probably couldn't have explained exactly why, as a matter of physiology, he could hit so many home runs. Nevertheless, he *could* hit them. Just as surely, the people whose examples I was following could triumph where most people failed—at art, at money, at advancement, at power, and at love and family.

Little by little, I started to share with others the knowledge that had worked so well for me. I wrote about it in newspaper and magazine articles, and even discussed it during television interviews.

I was still learning the secrets to success, and I hoped that others would want to learn, too. No one wants to be a failure, so readers and listeners did, in fact, show an interest in what I'd observed and had put into play. My theory was that if a man of reasonable care spent six years observing tennis professionals and reported that they had certain devices and practices that enabled them to ace their opponents nine times out of ten, and that he, a class-C player, had tried those tricks and had been able to ace his opponents eight times out of ten, tennis players would pay attention. Not everyone is a tennis player, but everyone plays at the sport of life. I was able to report how pros at the game did it so much more beautifully than we did, so people listened.

The listeners reported back to me that they found that my proposals worked in an astonishing variety of circumstances. The very rough guidelines that I offered helped people turn failure into success in marriage and in work. They lifted messengers and clerks into executive positions. They turned indolent, fearful retirement years into those marked by creative production and satisfaction.

The system I discovered was not a brainstorm that came to me while I was driving across a bridge, nor did I take it from the reading of psychological texts. The rules and suggestions I noted and used in my own life came from real-life, day-to-day observations of how successful people got that way. I couldn't claim to know how it was done when I started out. But after endless months of study, I had a pretty good idea. Like an anthropologist codifying the behavior of an exotic tribe, I'd studied the ways of those who'd gotten what they wanted from life. By adhering to their unusual methods, a person could actually become a member of that elegant tribe. So experience taught me.

※ ※ ※

I decided that in the interest of all those trapped in their own room 710 of the human spirit, and of those whose humanity was constantly being deadened by failure and frustration, I would set down on paper just what those rules were. I would share with anyone who cared to learn just how to get what they wanted out of life.

The attitudes and habits of thought I mention are not complex or mysterious. There's nothing of the conundrums of the East in these rules. Nor do I claim that one or two of these concepts have never occurred to you before. As a comprehensive plan for achievement of your dreams, however, they're recorded here for the first time (that I know of). Certainly, in their simplicity and inherent logic, they're uniquely accessible to most people.

So, for those of you who see your dreams receding, who know you could be more than you are, who take pride in your actions, and who see no reason why you should not have all that you want, here is the way to get it—through what I call . . . Bunkhouse Logic.

PART I

BUNKHOUSE LOGIC:
THE SPIRIT OF THE COWBOY

Bunkhouse Logic is easy to follow if you understand where its name comes from. Basically, a bunkhouse is where cowboys live. The logic of the bunkhouse is that which guides the cowboy's life. It's even more than logic, really, since it's the unspoken and unwritten code by which the cowboy must live every day if he is to accomplish anything at all.

The code, of course, involves all the tricky and complex aspects of life on a ranch or on the range. But it all comes under the headings of "Activity" and "Inner Mobility." The cowboy, who was once the symbol of this country in the eyes of its citizens, and who still *is* a cogent symbol of American life to foreigners, can't get anything done by sitting inside the bunkhouse and brooding. He can't get anything done by recalling past slights and how they've warped his character and spoiled his chances for happiness. The cowboy accomplishes nothing at all by staying in one place.

The cowboy, the quintessential American and inspiration to a planet, gets everything by movement and activity.

He must herd his cattle, making certain that he keeps ahead of them at some points and behind them at others. He must accept as routine the inclement weather: the rain, the heat, and the cold. He sees these elements not as personal enemies, but as facts of life to be endured and triumphed over. The recalcitrant calf is not an excuse for sulking. It's part of the environment—just like a rude and demanding boss or a vicious, officious receptionist would be. If a woodchuck appears and bites a calf, that doesn't require that the woodchuck be tortured and punished for what it has done, as if the rodent bore a personal grudge against the cowboy. It's simply an extremely good argument for moving the cattle somewhere else, just as a spouse who habitually acts abusively does not provide just cause for blood revenge, but is simply an argument for moving on.

The cowboy sees the perfection of his skills in wrangling, roping, herding, cutting, and so forth—not as justification for praise from his mommy and daddy, but instead as a means of survival in an uncompromising world. He knows that he can't sit in a dimly lit room and complain that he simply can't bring himself to go out on the range that day. He can and must ride, and the fact that he does so gives him the pride and the will to do it over and over again. This type of accomplishment leads to happiness.

The cowboy knows that when he has arrived at the edge of the prairie where a well has temporarily dried up, it does no good at all to sit by the dry hole and cry about it. The only thing to do is get on his horse and find a watering spot that's *not* dry. The cowboy would let his whole herd—and himself—die if he didn't keep moving. His mobility out there on the sagebrush trail is the exact equivalent of what you need to acquire in the city when you find that your job has turned out to be a dry hole. There's no sense at all in whining about it to anyone who will listen. The only thing that helps is finding water: the new job, the new city, the new girlfriend, the new opportunity for nurture and growth.

Of course, the kind of *geographic* mobility that the cowboy has so gracefully mastered on the prairie is not required or available or prudent in modern life. What is needed is *inner* mobility: the flexibility within your own head to realize that you've been doing something wrong, something that leads to obscurity, failure, low self-esteem, and unhappiness. You need the inner mobility to move on to new pastures, where you have a fighting chance of finding happiness and success in work, in love, at home—wherever you want it.

The logic of the bunkhouse requires constant activity, incessant mobility, and emphasis on performance—not excuses. All of this corresponds to an astonishing extent with the practices of the successful. By an extraordinary chance, the skills I observed at ranches in Montrose, Colorado; and Arvin, California, are amazingly similar to attributes I detected in the managing director of an investment bank and the CEO of Dow Jones, in the author of a best-selling saga and the producer of a top-grossing film.

Those same attitudes, the same set of values and practices, are carried around in the heads of financial wizards, as well as bronco-busting cowpokes in their Ford pickups. The stay-at-home moms who have, by sheer willpower, turned their marriages into temples of joy and refuge from the cruelty of the world, share the skills of the bull rider in Sheridan, Wyoming.

When you study these rules of Bunkhouse Logic, think of the American cowboy. Day after day he bets on himself to win—and he always collects the money. You'll have a better idea of what the rules entail if you keep him in mind.

Think of the cowboy caring for himself and his cattle in the largely hostile environment. He cannot possibly make his way unless he's active and inwardly mobile. When you contemplate a change in your life situation, and when you consider how many unknown and possibly dangerous factors there are in the world, think of the cowboy. He guides hundreds of cattle, each with a mind of its own, through a random and dangerous universe. He can do it because he is active and inwardly mobile—and you can be that way, too.

The cowboy faces a swollen stream. He realizes that he has to get across it somehow. That's you realizing that you have to do something dramatic to get yourself to the next level of the job even if it is risky. The cowboy faces the challenge by actively looking for a wider spot in the river where the water moves less dangerously. *You* will meet your challenge via the same tactics—activity and inner mobility.

The logic of the bunkhouse is varied and differs from situation to situation, but underlying it all are these two qualities. Think of the cowboy. He can teach you a lot. He's the romantic symbol of the successful in every area.

〰 〰 〰

PART II

BUNKHOUSE LOGIC:
WHAT IT IS AND WHAT IT IS NOT

We hold these truths to be self-evident:
In war there is no substitute for victory. In life there is
no substitute for happiness. The bare survival of each day,
dragging one's consciousness through misery, is not suf-
ficient redemption for the gift of being alive.

There is no happiness without self-esteem. What is it?
How do you get it? To be happy overall, one must be happy
with oneself. In real life, that comes from accomplishments
of which one can be proud. Getting a job that pays enough
for you to live like a princess is worth more than a thousand
hours of sitting in the Empire Room of the airport Holiday
Inn being told that you need do no more than "be yourself" to be happy. The human spirit needs to accomplish, to
achieve, to triumph, in order to be happy.

Low self-esteem is a feeling of dislike for yourself. It's
a sense that you're unworthy, undeserving, and generally
a mess. Low self-esteem invariably produces unhappiness.
Low self-esteem comes from failure and frustration. Once in
place, it becomes a paralyzing illness. It can and does hold
back people with great natural ability. It's a far more preva-
lent paralytic disease than multiple sclerosis. A woman sits

5

in her secretarial cubbyhole, knowing that she's as smart as the best-selling author she saw on *The Tonight Show.* She's also a virtual cinch to stay in her secretarial niche because years of being there have so devastated her self-esteem that she cannot ever write the book that might put her up there with Jay Leno.

High self-esteem can enable anyone to break out of any rut and move toward triumph. No matter what forces are arrayed against a man or woman with high self-esteem, he or she can defeat them. This is a self-fulfilling prophecy.

If you believe that the pitfalls and problems that beset every human being are easily surmounted by your ability and your strength, you will surmount them. If you believe that they are greatly in excess of your ability to attack them, they will defeat you. If the perpetual stumbling blocks to human happiness are seen as uniquely difficult and imposing, they will not be scaled. If you do not scale them, you remain in your situation of permanent, self-generating low self-esteem.

If you remain in your position of permanently low self-esteem, then you will never accomplish anything that gives you the pride and the energy to get out of the ditch you're in. Self-esteem will sink lower and lower until at last nothing can be accomplished. Getting out of bed each morning and going to work is a mammoth expedition, far more difficult than hiking to the South Pole. Making an appointment for dinner is like entering a Grand Prix of motorcycle racing. Changing the channel on the television is like charging up a hill at Gettysburg:

> Failure leads to low self-esteem.
>
> Low self-esteem leads to unhappiness.
>
> Low self-esteem and unhappiness are the two ineluctable handmaidens of a wasted life.

On the other hand, achievement leads to high self-esteem, which leads to more achievement, which leads to happiness.

The key to moving from the unhappiness cycle to the happiness cycle cannot be self-esteem in the first instance because self-esteem is dependent on achievement. The one and only way to break out of the cycle of low self-esteem and unhappiness is by achievement.

That is where Bunkhouse Logic comes in. It tells us how to stop failing and how to start achieving. Bunkhouse Logic is a complete and comprehensive plan of escape from the prison of failure. It's also a thorough and proven pathway to the highest rungs of success. Bunkhouse Logic is the set of attitudes that makes a person a success.

But bear in mind, Bunkhouse Logic is about how you face the challenges of daily life on a large scale. It is not about penmanship, speed-reading, calculus, or about balancing your checkbook. It is not about how to have a pleasant telephone manner, how to dress for success, or how to tune up your car yourself.

All those things are the details of life. They'll come automatically, if you want them, once you know how to act for success in general ways. A field marshal who has the plan for conquering France doesn't need to know the name of every restaurant in Tours. They're there if he wants them once he has the whole country.

An important point: Bunkhouse Logic takes fundamental issue with the power of psychiatry and psychology in today's world. To illustrate the difference in belief, I offer this example, drawn from the book of real life:

When I sat in my miserable room in the old *Star* building, a good friend came in to talk to me. I told him how desperately I wanted to get out of my life there and how miserably unhappy I was.

"The thing to do," he said, "is use the health insurance you have on this job to get ten years of psychoanalysis. Then when you're all better, you can go out and do something great."

That is the exact opposite of what I did. I took a wild stab that I would feel better if I first did something and then felt proud about myself. Accomplishment, however difficult, would come first. Then would come the happiness without which life is a shambles and a sham.

It is now many years later. My friend is still at the old *Star* building, at least psychologically. He occasionally leaves because of suicide attempts. Then he goes to Georgetown University Hospital for a time. He is now in his 40th year of psychoanalysis.

I do not for a moment question the value of psychotherapy for those who are mentally ill. But in today's world, far too many people with a vague sense of frustration and malaise waste their time sitting in dimly lit rooms talking about their childhoods to bored people who are contemplating their next real-estate venture. For a huge number of people, the ritual of psychotherapy is no more than an excuse for failure and unhappiness, a gesture of surrender to a difficult world, a cry for sympathy in the face of an uncompromising reality. For a large number of patients, the therapy process is a substitute for any concrete accomplishment in the world. The patient can always say that, after all, he's "trying."

Bunkhouse Logic says that instead of trying, *succeed.* Then see how much longer you feel like spending your valuable time talking to a stranger about your problems. Bunkhouse Logic says that even a small measure of real-life accomplishment is a far stronger benefit to the soul than any number of hours whining in a room lined with bookcases, modern art, and diplomas.

Certainly, for the genuinely ill, psychotherapy is crucial. But for the ordinary trapped, frustrated person, success is the cure for the blues.

Nor do you need to feel that before you can be successful, you must first be cured. The success is the cure. Go for it first, and the rest will follow.

Just before the Civil War, Jefferson Davis and Robert E. Lee had a conversation vaguely like this:

"Why don't you join us and lead the Confederate army?" Davis asked Lee.

"I don't feel fully committed," Lee said.

"Join first, and then you'll feel committed," Davis answered.

The Confederacy lost, but General Lee became one of the most admired generals of all time.

That is the spirit of Bunkhouse Logic. Act successfully and the emotional rewards will follow. Don't wait for a mysterious presence to enter you and guide you to nirvana. Do it now. Act and succeed, and nirvana will follow in due course.

〰 〰 〰

PART III

BUNKHOUSE LOGIC: RANDOM NOTES BEFORE YOU START

Risk is the key to everything. The venture that doesn't involve risk possesses only the most minimal possibility of achieving success. It's a cardinal principle of all investment and speculation matters that the greatest likelihood of gain on a substantial scale occurs in enterprises with the greatest risk of loss. In the world of moneymaking endeavors, there's the safe way—putting money into a savings account, which yields 4 percent. Then there's the speculation in commodities contracts, which often yields 100 percent in a day. The savings account is perfectly safe against loss, while the commodities contract is dangerous. You can lose every penny in a minute (and I don't recommend it, except as an analogy).

The risk premium is actually a factor in every area of life. The girl who sat next to you in your high school homeroom and has always had a crush on you is perfectly safe, but she doesn't seem like much of a challenge. However, the girl who makes men walk into walls is a potential heartbreaker, but the night she tells you that she loves you is the biggest night of your life.

The job you have—the one that doesn't pay you enough to cover your monthly payments on your Sears credit card and which features secretaries who snicker at you when you ask them to take a message—is yours for life. It's safe and secure. But it's not the stuff of dreams. It offers no risk, but also no return.

On the other hand, the job you want, the one where you can make it onto the executive jet overnight, will require you to take a few risks. You may have to dream up a completely new approach for how to run your department, and you may have to challenge the competence of your superiors, knowing that if you fail, the risks will be great. But if you succeed, you can feel that you've done something great with your formerly failed life.

To succeed in the real world, you sometimes have to step off the train completely and wait at the station until the right one comes along. You may have to quit your salaried job and live hand-to-mouth for a time. You may have to move out of your nice house and live in a small studio apartment for a while. And you may have to work for yourself so that your earnings depend entirely on your own exertions and your own success. But that success may not come for a while. You may find yourself eating Hamburger Helper more than hamburgers. But when the break does come, it can come in a big way, unimpeded by your old boss and your old job and your old limits. You will have made it onto the right track, the right job, and the right level of creativity for you. The rewards will be far richer than they ever could have been without the risk.

Bunkhouse Logic must always be undertaken with the idea that risk is inevitable, healthy, and desirable, and you may find yourself questioning whether you can tolerate so much uncertainty and possibility of failure. The answer is that: (1) The choice is between the risk of success and the certainty of failure if you do not take the Bunkhouse Logic advice; and (2) there is no success without risk, so there really is no choice if you want to get the things you've always wanted.

Bunkhouse Logic is a continuing process for getting what you want at all stages of your progress through life. It's not only for getting off the floor. It's also for breaking through the ceiling.

Since Bunkhouse Logic is the codification of the rules by which the successful get what they want, it's useful at every stage of your transit through life. It's just as useful in learning how to go from the $50,000-a-year level to the millionaire level as it is in getting the first job. It's as fully applicable to the move from columnist to popular-culture baron as it is to the move from day worker to lady of the house, or the move from college graduation to captain of industry.

One of the most interesting facts of life is that once you've put yourself on the track toward getting what you want, no one tucks you into a comfortable bed and carries you toward your destination while you curl up reading *Barron's* or *Fortune.* You have to work to get off the wrong track onto the right track, and then you have to work to keep *moving* on that track. Your momentum will carry you only a few days or months at most. To succeed takes constant effort, unstinting and unending.

Popular mythology tells us that some waitress is discovered while humming a tune. The next thing she knows she has a home on Park Avenue and a lifetime contract with a record company. The office boy makes a suggestion to his boss about how to make a cheaper widget and the next thing he knows he's living on ten acres in McLean, Virginia.

It doesn't work like that. Success is an incremental, step-by-step process in which you work your way up the ladder millimeter by millimeter, pushing all the time. The guides for successful action contained in this book are not only useful, but also absolutely necessary at every step of the journey to your heart's destination. If you happen to discover the principles of Bunkhouse Logic when you're already two-thirds of the way there, it will make your remaining trip much easier. If you happen to pick up this book when your goal is a million miles away, take comfort. It's always a step-by-step journey for everyone. Bunkhouse Logic will be there with you every step of the way, like an old friend.

It ain't easy to succeed, but it's easier than failing. Put another way, Bunkhouse Logic in no way promises you that the road to getting what you want out of life is effortless downhill skiing. Far from it. Betting on yourself and winning takes persistence, endurance, and trouble. It requires strength to stay on top of the game and to play to win. To get what you want requires constant, unending application of the maxims of the bunkhouse. Sometimes that will hurt, but it will hurt a lot less than it would to not get what you want out of life.

Finally, do it now. No amount of brooding about the meaning of life or about the meaning of Bunkhouse Logic will take the place of actually getting out of your shell, your office, your home, or your apartment and going out into real life and spreading your wings. Thought is essential. Psychic preparation is essential. But they're both slow suicide if they take the place of activity in the real world.

You must take that first step off the diving board in order to learn how to dive. You must make that first telephone call or go to that first meeting or address your adversary that first time to get the Bunkhouse Logic process on the road. The first steps will take some effort, maybe pain. But after that, everything that has to be done is real-life movement.

This book is organized into five parts. The first four (three of which you've already read) tell you how to get ready to play the game of getting what you want from life. It prepares you to step up to the table where life's possibilities are passed out. The fifth part tells you how the game is played. It lays out the rules that successful people use to win. These rules will enable *you* to win, too.

\|/ \|/ \|/

PART IV

PREPARING FOR THE GAME

1. DECIDE WHAT YOU WANT

Trips and Destinations

The indispensable first step to getting the things you want out of life is this: Decide what you want.

Picture the cowboy. He awakens one morning somewhere west of Laramie and climbs out of his sleeping bag. Around him are hundreds of milling cattle munching on sage grass. He knows that he has to get those cattle to market. If he does, he'll collect a bonus from the trail boss. The cowboy knows something fundamental: If he's ever going to get those cattle to market, he must first know where the market is.

He doesn't wake up and say to himself, *Gee, maybe I'll take the cattle to St. Louis. Or maybe I'll take them to Chicago. On the other hand, I hear that Kansas City is nice.*

Far from it. He knows that he has to have those cattle at a certain railway junction on the outskirts of Sheridan by the next morning. That's his first major step toward getting them there—he knows their destination.

This is not as obvious as it sounds. How many times have people asked you what you want to be doing five years from now? How many times have you been able to give them a sensible answer? It is no answer at all to say, "I want to be happy" or "I want to be somebody important." Those are not destinations of achievement. Those are desired states of mind that you can reach after you've made good on your goals.

The cowboy knows this in his bones. He knows that to be happy, he must get those cattle to market. He knows without thinking about it that *reaching* his destination will be impossible without *knowing* his destination.

That knowledge is largely unknown among vast numbers of people today. They simply do not know what they want out of life. How can they possibly expect to get where they want to go if they don't know where that is?

To reiterate, in order to make any progress at all toward a destination, one must know what that destination is. Suppose that you had a gnawing wish to go on a vacation to some spot far beyond your normal perambulations. You know that you want it to be sunny and cheerful, with a wide sandy beach and a bar nearby with lots of banana daiquiris. But you know that there are many such places in the world. There's Aruba and Martinique and Florida and Puerto Vallarta and Mazatlán and Singapore and Morocco and Nassau and Bermuda and Sea Island, and hundreds if not thousands more. You have your American Express card and you're ready to go. But you *can't* go because you haven't decided which resort you're headed for.

You call the travel agent to map out a route in vain because you have no idea where you want to wind up. The airlines can spit out hundreds of combinations of alluring airfares, but that does no good at all. You can't take advantage of any fares because you simply have no idea where you want to go. So you stay where you are, and another vacation goes by with you sitting in your bedroom watching MTV instead of relaxing on the beach.

Again, we're talking about the exact analogue of human life. Yes, you get up in the morning and wonder why a cruel fortune placed you where you are—in the file room or tenth in line for the sales manager's job or analyzing spreadsheets year after year—and you know that you want to be somewhere better. But to take the crucial first steps toward getting to that better place, you must have a good idea of where that place is.

Look at it in another way. To cure a disease, the doctor must first diagnose it successfully. So if you call him up, you tell him what's wrong. You want him to know what your body needs, whether it be medicine, therapy, surgery, or the entire panoply of medical weapons.

You don't go to the doctor and say, "Hey, I don't feel so good. Please make me feel great." You and the doctor must put together all the facts at your disposal to allow the medical machinery to work its magic upon you.

The cure cannot possibly be found until the disease is found.

In life, you often walk around sick with unhappiness and frustration. To get well, you have to know what the disease is: Lack of being the boss in your workplace? Lack of a gorgeous blue-eyed girlfriend? Lack of a degree in anthropology? Lack of a million dollars?

To find the cure for life's ailments, you must know what those ailments are. In other words, you must know what you want out of life. Then you can proceed to get it. Once you've diagnosed what you need from life, then you're on your way.

The ancient Greek heroes accomplished a great many mythical feats. They slew giants and crossed stormy seas and wrestled with the gods. They did a great many things that you might consider impossible. But they had a leg up on any of us because they'd all had their destinies pointed out to them. Once their fate was clear, they were freed from the necessity of spending any further time on actions and deeds extraneous to their path.

None of us is Theseus, but the principle is the same. You can waste an enormous, pitiful amount of time unless you know where you want to go. But once you do know where you want to go, anything is possible.

Dreaming and Thinking

This all leads to an important unanswered question: *How do you know what you want?* How do you decide which of the life opportunities that shower you with their promises are the ones you should pursue? If you've gotten confused about which of life's goals you want to pursue, how do you get straightened out and follow the path to one lone pot of gold?

There are several answers to that tricky question. First, consult your dreams. Try to remember the most vivid sleeping dreams that made you the most euphoric. What were you doing in those dreams? In what way did you spend your time in those sleeping moments of pride and contentment? For many people, a dream recurs night after night.

There the deepest wishes of the human spirit are unearthed. In those reveries are the best clues to what you want to do during this brief earthly transit. In your most unrestrained moments, dreaming tells you what you would do if you could do anything.

Of course, some dreams will be fantastic and simply impossible, such as dreaming that you're the head of the Mayan empire. And other dreams will involve unending sexual activity, which isn't a possibility for most people who have to earn a living or care for a family. But even those dreams give you a clue about the direction that your one and only goal should take. If you have dreams of being the reincarnation of Alexander the Great or of having a marathon night with the athletic team of your choice, you're longing for power and the opportunity for wide sexual contacts. Lighthouse keeper or nun would probably not be the right goal. Treat your dreams as a guide to what you must decide you want, even if in general terms.

Cato the Censor, the great moral guardian of republican Rome, preached and shouted against the decline of morality until he had a repetitive dream. He could see the Carthaginian legions sacking Rome. He turned every talent he had to speaking out in favor of Rome attacking Carthage. He ended every speech in the Senate by saying, ". . . et Carthago delenda est," which means "and my further opinion is that Carthage must be destroyed." Soon Carthage was leveled and its ground sown with salt.

On a more domestic level, one of the women at my bank in Los Angeles used to buttonhole me whenever she saw me at her teller window. She told me of her dream where she was sitting behind an immense desk, barking out orders to her own secretaries. She had that dream over and over again, and now she's in charge of a hiring program at Boeing, sitting behind a huge desk, barking out orders.

But dreams can be diffuse. Just as a man or woman can have many idylls of glory in many different fields, so she or he can have the same kinds of fantasies while sleeping, so that no narrowing of focus is achieved at all.

In that case, a retrospective study of childhood daydreams is often useful. In case after case of talking to the successful about what they wanted to do with their lives when they were ten years old, I've found that they're doing just that today. The long summer-afternoon wishes of childhood cast a lingering spell over life. If you can delve into your memory, find those dreams. You may discover that they still tell you what you want to do with your life as an adult. The thoughts of youth are long thoughts, as the saying goes. They can be just as useful for the future as the past. Let them tell you what you really want.

There's also the simple, rational process of thinking carefully about what you'd genuinely like to be doing if you could do anything. Try this: Take out a yellow legal pad and sit in your living room with no distractions. Make a list of the alternatives you've decided you're interested in. Put the attributes of the goals that most attract you and those that most repel you on the list. Think about what it would be like to actually be there—to have the vice presidency for new development, to be married to the most beautiful girl with the sweetest smile, to live in a cabin in the middle of the Rockies without any neighbors within sight. Feel which of the alternatives moves you the most. If one of them genuinely gets your blood flowing, that's the one you have to go for.

One of my college roommates was planning to go to law school, and he did. About ten years later, he was miserable in his work at a New York City law firm that specialized in mergers and acquisitions. He was an ordinary fellow, and he simply listed on a pad of paper all the possibilities for a new life that had occurred to him as he lifted his eyes from tender-offer documents. As he went through the list, he came upon one that actually made his skin tingle with excitement. Now he teaches history at a boarding school in New Hampshire. I've rarely seen a happier man.

The Uses of Envy

There's another extremely valuable tool available for helping you decide what you really want: envy. In one of those rare situations where a vice can be turned into a virtue, envy can be turned to your advantage. It can help you understand just what your deepest wishes are for yourself.

Imagine that you're in your living room one night watching a rerun of *Seinfeld.* The telephone rings just as Kramer bursts through Jerry's door. You pick up the telephone. It's your best friend Ray calling to tell you that Gary, a man who rides to work with you in your car pool, has just been promoted to the job of visiting supervisor of all the branches of your company in the Southwest. You burn with envy. You've always wanted to spend more time in that part of the country. You can hardly control yourself. When you get back to the TV, you can hardly concentrate on the flickering images of Jerry and his friends bickering.

Something wasteful and painful is going on here—envy. It's eating up your peace of mind, destroying your self-confidence. But it's also definitely doing something positive for you. It's telling you that you want to do the same kind of thing that your friend Gary is doing. If his new job were not penetrating some deep well of longing within your own personality, you'd never experience the pain you do upon hearing of his good fortune. Your envy doesn't mean that you're a bad person or a criminal. But it does mean that Gary has something you want. It may not be everything. You may want only the Southwest without the job, or you may want the job without the Southwest. But he's doing you the favor of clarifying in your mind just what you want.

One of my old high school classmates married while in college and had two children. By the time she was in her 30s, her children were in their teens and her financial situation was good enough for her to afford a maid in her suburban Philadelphia home. Basically, she had the opportunity to try a whole new kind of life. At first she thought she'd become a real-estate broker. "I just thought I'd do that because I knew that was what a lot of women were doing," she said. "But I decided that life was too short to spend in the real-estate business." So she tried to become a dress designer. "That was another thing women did in the city—and I thought we were close enough to Philadelphia to be in 'the city.' So I made a few dresses and took them to stores in my area. At first everyone turned me down," she continued. "Once a manager offered to buy my whole line—but only if I'd go with him to a motel—so that line of work was out."

The woman in question still had the money and leisure to try again, but she didn't know where to go. Then one day it was all clarified. "I was at lunch with some friends, and one of the girls said she'd just gotten a job in planning for Dynasciences, a big electronics company. She got to review all the other division's plans and approve or disapprove them. When I got home," my friend told me, "I was so angry I couldn't see straight. I'd been kicked all over creation by punks and lechers, and she was going to have this secure job where she got to pass on and maybe reject other people. *I* had been the rejected one, and now she was going to be rejecting people. It was really annoying. That was how I knew I wanted to be a manager, reviewing other people's work at a big company. I wanted to be in the catbird seat, not in the defendant's box."

The woman went to The Wharton School at the University of Pennsylvania and took classes preparing her to examine plans for the expansion of utilities. Now she works for a major electric company, and no one can say "Boo!" without consulting her. She's in seventh heaven. Her envy guided her to the path that would truly make her happy in life.

Of course, envy is a blunt instrument. If a friend lands a high-paying, glamorous job with a great office in a fine part of town, you're likely to feel envy. But you may not be able to tell for certain what part of the picture generates this emotion—as in the case of the supervisor in the Southwest. So the raw emotion of envy will have to be sharpened considerably by your own rational process of elimination.

The creative vice president of a major advertising agency told me how he required two steps of envy to show him his goal. "When I was in college," he recalled, "I envied the English professors. They just seemed to have the perfect jobs, sitting in offices all day thinking about poetry. So I went to graduate school and studied English poetry of the late Victorian era. It was so boring that I felt like throwing up whenever I opened the books."

He quit graduate school and went to work for DDB Needham, a major advertising agency. "That was it. It wasn't studying literature that I envied. It was the way professors seemed to just hang around all day thinking of clever things to say. Now I do that in an office on the 30th floor of the General Motors Building. The clever things I make up are about detergent, but I love them anyway. I love just looking out my window, thinking. That was what I really envied."

So please do not disregard envy as a positive force for improvement. It can tell you what you really want from life.

The Escape Hatch

Life is filled with surprises. You go out to eat thinking that you're dying to have some ravioli stuffed with cheese, and with it, you want a green salad with Tuscan dressing. Alas, when the meal is put in front of you and you take that first taste, you find that what you really wanted was a center-cut New York strip steak. But there you are at the Villa Torino, and you're with a party of five who are having a heavenly time with their veal Florentine.

You think that your heart's desire is to live in a house by the ocean. Just thinking of the waves on the shore and the sun setting above the sea puts you in a mood of pure heaven-sent bliss. You can just imagine that a day spent by the water will be one free of travail and heartache, filled richly to the brim with joy and fulfillment. You spend years searching for that perfect beach house. At last you find it, and it's wonderful—perfection in wood, stone, and glass. You gather every cent you have for the down payment and you move in. But that first evening at the beach, you find yourself crawling with anxiety. Where are the bright lights of the city? Where's the fun and music and fine food?

Life is full of little twists. You can even take a wrong turn once you've followed the first rule of Bunkhouse Logic: *Decide what you want.* It's entirely possible that you'll decide that your heart's desire is to be a chemical engineer, only to discover that your real aim is to be a poet. You've gotten yourself high up within DuPont, only to find that you want to be in a cabin in Naugatuck, contemplating a pond and writing rhymed verse about it.

After all of your careful consultation of your dreams, your childhood fantasies, your realistic and rational joys and pains, and your envy, you've made a decision: You hate working in a bank. Or you hate working in a hospital. Or you hate being married. Or you hate living alone.

No problem. After all, the key underlays of the logic of the bunkhouse are neither more nor less than inner mobility and activity. If you find that you cannot muster the enthusiasm necessary to take you where you want to go, you owe it to yourself to find the right goal that will summon up the requisite energy and willpower to move you forward. There's absolutely no point at all in staying in a job or personal situation that turns out to be wrong for you. When you get on the wrong track, every stop is the wrong stop. Just get off that track, pronto. Use your inner mobility and get moving.

You'll know if you're doing the right thing and heading in the right direction if you're eager to pursue your goal and if you regret the time you spend away from that pursuit. When you're ready to spring out of bed to move along the path to what you want, then you're on the right track.

Use your envy, your dreams, your fantasies, and your inner mobility to decide what you want. Then go forward with confidence to the next steps of Bunkhouse Logic.

2. Ask for What You Want

Now that you've decided what you want, the next of many steps is to ask for it. It will never come your way unless you do.

No Answers Without Prayers

One of the most persistent myths of modern life goes something like this: In the small town of Mapleville, Ohio, lives beautiful Lesley Anne Innocent. Lesley Anne is a shy girl who almost never goes out of the white clapboard house in which she lives with her father, the town pharmacist, and her mother, who's active in the Junior League. Lesley Anne spends most of her time reading biographies of Marie Antoinette and Mary, Queen of Scots. The rest of the time she crochets and helps her mother around the house.

Lesley Anne has confided in her best friend, Letitia, that her greatest ambition is to become a movie star and play the roles of great historical women. Of course, she's far too shy to ever do anything about it. Still, it's what she dreams about while sleeping on her Ethan Allen maple bed.

One day, Michael Worth, a powerful Hollywood producer, drives through town in his Ferrari Luso on the way to visit his aging grandmother in Oakville, 20 miles up the road. He stops at the Mapleville Diner for a piece of their famous pie. Unfortunately, while he gulps down the pie, he gets a stomachache. He's out of Lomotil, so he goes to the Mapleville Pharmacy to buy some Kaopectate.

While there, he strikes up a conversation with John Innocent, pharmacist and father of Lesley Anne Innocent.

Both men are interested in Coca-Cola advertisements from the 19th century. After John has calmed down Michael's stomach, he takes the producer down the streets of Mapleville to his house to see his collection of turn-of-the-century Coca-Cola artifacts. As they drive down the shady streets in Michael's roadster, Michael tells John Innocent that he probably got his stomachache because he was so aggravated about not being able to find the lead for the new multibillion-dollar Universal epic, *The Great Queens of Europe.* None of the established leading ladies is quite right for the part. There are no ingenues who really know the roles of the queens down to their fingertips. The role should go to someone new, beautiful, and deeply interested in the subject.

At that moment, they pull up to the Innocent home in Mapleville. By coincidence, Lesley Anne has just finished crocheting a medieval wool dress like the one Mary, Queen of Scots wore when she was beheaded. She's walking outside in her new outfit, reading a book under the shade of the maple trees. When Michael sees her, his heart leaps. There in little Mapleville is the girl, the one and only girl, the cosmic girl for the part.

By pleas and entreaties, Michael takes Lesley Anne off to Hollywood, where she lives chastely in a $26 million house off Sunset Boulevard. She's a natural talent and quickly becomes the leading lady of Hollywood, learning the ways of the rich and the powerful, but maintaining her maidenly ways of humility.

The Great Queens of Europe grosses $575 million domestically. And so the story goes.

Forget about it. This idea of getting your dreams to come true by accident is a fantasy. Once you've decided what you want, you must ask and ask and ask for it.

In real life, the story of Lesley Anne Innocent would be that if she spent all of her time in Mapleville, reading books about famous queens of history, she would probably wind up in the county mental hospital. At best, she'd live out her life in complete obscurity, her fantasies her only company as she passed down the one-way street of life. She would far more likely wind up as a Tennessee Williams protagonist than a Horatio Alger character. Like all people who fail to ask for what they want, she would *not* get what she wanted.

On earth, to him who asks shall it be answered. No other dispensations are allowed. The secret ambition, the concealed desire for something new and wonderful and satisfying remains secret, concealed, and unfulfilled. To get it, whatever it is, you must always ask for it.

Nevertheless, the infantile fantasy dies hard. The world is filled with junior salesmen who have a fantasy of becoming the owner of their own business. The typing pools of America are bursting with women who dream of designing clothes for Donna Karan. And the commuter trains are filled with accountants who vividly wish for life on a Wyoming ranch. They dream their dreams, wish their wishes, and fantasize in silence, telling their dreams to friends and relations over a few drinks, but they do no more.

Bunkhouse Logic tells you the hard and simple truth that if you fail to ask for what you want, you'll suffer its absence in silence for as long as you live. It's only in fairy tales, novels, and Hollywood movies that wishes come true simply from wishing. It will not happen to you. In real life, successful people, those who get what they want out of life, ask for those things over and over again.

There are many different ways to ask. The most straightforward is to say in a loud voice: "I want that!" But there are other ways as well. Some of them come under the heading of asking by doing.

Example: You're at a law firm, working as a junior associate on a case involving regulations for manufacturing cardboard shipping cartons. You're so bored that you hardly know what to do with yourself. Each day you pore over the Federal Register studying new rules about the thickness and corrugation of the brown cardboard boxes. You want to be working on exciting, large-scale antitrust cases, litigating with the big guns of Wall Street, putting your skills to work on life-or-death matters for giant corporations.

As a first step, you go to the partner who handles antitrust litigation. You tell him that you'd like to be included in the team working on the XYZ Corporation antitrust matter. He smiles at you past his $400 loafers, which he has propped up on his desk. "Thanks for making yourself available," he says. And that is very likely to be the end of it unless you add some work into the mixture.

If you go to that partner and tell him that you want to work on the XYZ Corporation antitrust team and that you've been doing a little reading in your spare time, and you then launch into a complicated and comprehensive discussion of all the relevant antitrust cases, including some so recent that the partner hasn't heard of them, and if you go into a lengthy statement about the economic underpinnings of the case, showing a depth of knowledge that few people outside MIT might have, you will get on the XYZ antitrust team as sure as there's sunshine in Los Angeles.

Of course, that will mean that you have to spend some extra hours hitting the books and perhaps even interviewing people, but that shouldn't be a problem. If you've decided that antitrust litigation is what you want, then 100 hours of extra legal research to get into the field is child's play. The work creates the expertise, which in turn makes for a meaningful request for what you really want.

Example: You're sick to death of living in the pollution and dirt of the big city. You want your husband to pick up and move to a small town in Vermont. There, you and he can begin a new, simpler life. It will have the kind of scope that allows time for love and tenderness while the city folks fight traffic.

You go to your hubby and say, "Hubby, let's move to Huddlesfield. We could have a swell life there."

It would be extremely likely that your hubby would say, "Are you kidding? You know how long it took me to get to assistant sales manager at the plant? You know how much of a cut in pay I'd have to take? Plus, our friends are here."

You have now asked in a simple, childish way. If you really want to move to Huddlesfield, you prepare to ask in more effective ways. You collect pictures of how pretty Huddlesfield looks in the snow. You get data about how much cheaper life would be there. You send away for pictures of beautiful, romantic cottages in the pines. You take long weekends near and in Huddlesfield. You find out about jobs in that little town so that you can tell your hubby that you'd actually be economically better off in Huddlesfield— or only slightly worse off. You get articles about how the pace of city life kills people at a young age.

In a word, you ask by doing. You ask in a way that gives you a high likelihood of getting what you want in the form of a positive response.

Letting Others Know

There's a danger that once you've decided what you want and have done some perfunctory asking for it, you'll then think that you've let the world know what you want. You might imagine that the world is informed of your wants and needs and will therefore be able to rush out and make sure that your dreams come true.

Not so. You may know what you want, but the people around you—those who can help make your dreams come to fruition—do not necessarily know. A lot of people take a lot of telling to learn something simple . . . like what you want out of life.

If you want people to know what you want, be prepared to sound like an advertisement for Tums. Go in and hit them with it over and over again. Lack of repetition, excessive subtlety—these things can keep you from making your wishes known. Of course, you don't want to sound like a whining baby, but you do want the people who count to get the message. Be sweet. Be gentle. Be polite. But let the message get out clearly.

The Key Person Is You

If there were such a thing as a built-in alarm that would go off when you, the reader, neared a crucial place in a book, one would go off here. Flashing red lights; a wailing siren; soaring, exploding fireworks; dazzling bursts of flame and sound—all would come into play.

Those alarms would announce a desperately important, easily overlooked fact of Bunkhouse Logic: The main person to ask for what you want is *you*.

You can ask for what you want from all kinds of people in your life. You can ask for a promotion from a boss. You can ask for a film contract from a producer. You can ask for a loan from a bank. You can ask for a pardon from the governor.

All of those people may be able to help.

But the only person who really matters is you. You're the one who must put forth the effort. You're the one who must concentrate her energies. You must make the total commitment. All that you ask for from someone else you must ask for a hundredfold, a thousandfold, from yourself.

If you have your own personal commitment to achieving your goals, you cannot fail to meet them. The most powerful magnates, the most learned professors, the most charismatic men and women, and the most encouraging parents can be approached with your requests. But their answers are irrelevant unless you've already given that totally committed answer to your own questions.

Once there was a beautiful flight attendant with magnificent dark blue eyes, the kind that would make men kill for her. She had lovely lips and a flashing smile. In a word, she was gorgeous. She had a quick mind and always said the right things. She made men fall in love with her at a frantic clip. Her abilities were overwhelmingly wasted in serving drinks and roast-beef slices to the people in first class, or chicken in little plastic containers to the passengers in coach.

A producer approached her with a suggestion. "You," he said, "are a personality genius. You are also attractive, even seductive. You should be a media superstar. I can help make it happen. I *will* make it happen."

"Really?" the flight attendant asked. "Really?"

"Absolutely," the producer said. "All you have to do is give up flying for a few months and get to know people in Hollywood. You don't have to sleep with them. All you have to do is let them know what kind of personality whiz kid you are."

"Three months?" she asked.

"That's all. Just three months. I don't think it would even take that long," the producer said.

"Gosh," the flight attendant said, "I really want to be a media superstar. I really do. Can't you arrange it for me so that I won't have to take off that much time? I'm supposed to spend some time on a boat off Long Beach with my boyfriend, a wealthy contractor who's already given me two gold watches. He told me I could have anything I want."

That was two years ago. The flight attendant is now married to the wealthy contractor in Long Beach. When she watches television, she cries. "I could have done that," she sobs. "I really could have. Now, it's a big day for me if I go out and play canasta with the ladies at the tennis club. I could kill myself right on the spot."

The flight attendant, who had every bit of natural talent to make it in a major way, asked the producer to give her what she really wanted. But she didn't ask herself. She refused to make the demands upon herself that would have guaranteed a successful life. If she'd asked herself for what she really wanted, she would surely have gotten it. She did not ask, and she did not get.

There was once a lawyer who worked night and day for large corporate clients. She defended them in difficult and painful trade-regulation cases. Her weekends were filled with research, and her nights were spent drafting over a hard table. She lost her enthusiasm as her youth ebbed into endless suffering on behalf of a giant corporation.

She was a beautiful woman with high cheekbones and graceful, soaring eyebrows. Her chin was perfection in a chin. Her hair was a stunning burnt auburn. Her voice was filled with warmth and kindness. When she smiled, she looked like a goddess.

All of that—all of that youth, beauty, and enthusiasm—was thrown into an immense corporate receptacle that consumed it without leaving a trace. The lawyer didn't like her life. Her girlish dreams of a life of walking through castles and English country homes had turned into a reality of endless 7 A.M. meetings with expert witnesses who reeked of gin.

"I want out," she said. "I desperately want out."

A way presented itself: She could leave work and travel the world in a carefree way if she could get a certain man to marry her. But, as it happened, that man was her ex-husband, and he was currently living with another woman. The man was neurotic and erratic beyond words, but the lawyer loved him. She wanted to remarry him, make him sane, and then have him take her around to castles and English country homes.

The effort would require enormous concentration. It would entail inevitable setbacks. She asked, in a moment of crisis, whether she could make that effort. She didn't ask her ex-husband whether he wanted to remarry her. She asked *herself* whether she would make the effort to plunge into the battle to change her life by leaving the practice of law and remarrying her former husband.

The woman decided that she would do all that was necessary to win back her ex, make him straighten up and fly right, and have him take her all around the world to castles and English country houses.

It took three years of relentless travail. First, the girl-friend was disposed of. Then the ex-husband's aversion to marriage was conquered. Finally, the ex-husband was induced to leave Los Angeles and travel to castles and English country houses while still supporting his wife and himself in an elegant style.

At this moment, the woman is one of the world's acknowledged experts on English country houses. "Every day is a picnic," she says, "a beautiful holiday. And so different from what I was afraid my life would be. I'm the luckiest girl in the world."

The flight attendant would ask someone else to make her a star, but she would not ask herself for the major sacrifices that were required. The lawyer *would* ask herself, answering in the affirmative, and she did win the life she wanted.

Bunkhouse Logic assures you that if you ask yourself for what you want, and if you answer yes, that key response will unlock the doors.

The Cowboy Again

Once again, think of that great American archetype, the cowboy. He has his cattle out there wandering around in a large herd. He has to have them in Abilene by nightfall. That's his job. He won't get paid unless he does it.

He must do two very simple and direct things once he knows where he wants to go. He must ask the trail boss for the necessary pickup trucks, fellow cowpokes, tents, meals, portable radios, prods, and everything else necessary to make the trip. Far more important, he must ask himself to go to Abilene with the cattle. If he doesn't take that perfectly obvious step of agreeing with himself to go, he'll never get to Abilene. Those cattle will forever meander about aimlessly. And he'll lose his job.

So without even thinking clearly about it, we must do the exact same thing. We must ask of others what we need for our lives. Much more important, we must ask ourselves for what we want.

Don't Ask for What You Don't Want

All the parts of the action rule *Ask for what you want* are important. The "what you want" part is particularly key. It simply means that you should not ask for what someone else wants. You must ask for what *you* personally want.

Everyone is subject to others' opinions. That is the nature of life in society. Your mother tells you what you should do. Your father tells you what you should do. So do your brothers and sisters. So do your friends. So do your teachers, newspapers, television shows, movies, books, records, plays, and everything else that touches your life in an expressive way.

The poor child who wants to play the violin is instead handed a baseball glove by his father or an electron microscope by his mother. The adult who might be perfectly happy whiling away his hours as a clerk in an obscure department is told that he must instead become a star of stage and screen. The woman who would like to be a captain of industry is brainwashed into thinking that she wants to be a housewife, or vice versa. Everyone has an idea for how you should spend your life.

That's fine for them. But if they send you off on a year-long errand that turns out to be entirely wrong for you, who suffers? The advice-giver goes merrily on with his life. He hasn't wasted one moment of his time. You, on the other hand, have invested your time and lost every bit of the gamble.

You must, must, must, without fail, ask only for what you want. You must not make the mistake of asking for what you do not want, or for what someone else wants for you.

It's your life. None of the advice-givers, none of the career-steerers, can give you back one instant of the time they took away by their bad advice.

You have only one absolutely limited quantity in your life: time. No one can give you any more time than your incredibly brief lifetime gives you. No matter what you do in this world, you cannot alter your allotted span of time. Once it's gone, it's really gone.

No one—not Martha Stewart, not Michael Jordan, not Bill Gates, not Jack Nicholson—no one can have an infinite supply of time. It runs out for all of us—and soon, too.

It's a cardinal rule of life that you should not waste it. Bunkhouse Logic gives you a further cardinal rule that says that you shouldn't waste one instant of it asking for what you do not want.

It will be possible to get all you want out of life; Bunkhouse Logic charts the path. But it will certainly not be possible if you're constantly running off on other people's errands. If you waste your precious lifetime asking for what other people want, you'll never get the things *you* want.

Life is short, so make it sweet by going for what you want and not for what someone else wants. *Don't ask for what you don't want* applies to all areas of life: personal career, creative, romantic, family matters—everything. Waste is the enemy of success. Bunkhouse Logic begs you not to waste the only life you have by chasing after things, people, or situations that you don't really want.

From the first action rule—*Decide what you want*—you know what you desire. Go for it and not for anything else. Ride your own merry-go-round. Stay off your mother's or *Time* magazine's or *Vogue*'s.

Life's Role Model Agency

Just as you shouldn't follow the advice of people who don't know or respect your deepest wishes, you should and must have role models. If you find someone who lives the kind of life you'd like to live, follow that person's life and imitate it. Imitation, as every psychology student knows, is a form of learning. In fact, for many people, it's the most valuable form. Babies imitate those who walk—and they walk. They imitate those who talk—and they talk.

When you decide what you want out of life, you'll probably be helped in making your decision by envy, as recounted in the section on deciding what you want. There will likely be someone who is the object of your envy, whose life you'd like to lead. Do not scorn or reject that person because of envy. Learn from her. Imitate him.

So part of asking for what you want is to definitely have a role model. You figure out what it is about a particular person that you want to duplicate, then you ask yourself— and others—for the things and the qualities he or she has. Later in this book, there will be more about role models in other action rules and rules of thought, but for the time being, please remember: It's normal, healthy, and desirable to have a role model. But the role model must truly be *your* role model, in that he or she can teach you exactly what to ask for, how to ask, and how to play the game. But a role model foisted upon you by someone else is not at all useful. Indeed, asking to be like such a person is simply another aspect of waste—the mortal enemy of success.

Summing Up

- Once you've decided what you want, you must ask for it with activity and inner mobility.

- You must ask at the proper time and place, which will give you the best shot at getting what you want.

- You must ask so that other people will know what you want.

- You must ask yourself primarily for what you want. *Your* answer is the key answer.

- You must ask not only by talking, but also by doing.

- You must stay off other people's merry-go-rounds. It's possible to get all that you want, but only if you don't waste your time seeking other people's goals as if they're your own. You must ask for what you want, and not for what someone else wants.

- You must not avoid role models. You should seek to find out what they have that you want in order to know what to ask for.

- Ask for what you want!

3. You Can't Win if You're Not at the Table

The Casino of Life

If all of the meaning inherent in Bunkhouse Logic had to be condensed into a single sentence, that statement would be: "You can't win if you're not at the table." Into those nine words is packed an infinitude of wisdom that bears upon why the successful are that way, and why others are the way *they* are.

Back in the summer of 1973, during the lowest days of my life, after I'd determined that I had to break out of room 710 of the old *Star* building, I sat in a secondhand armchair with green cotton upholstery, reading by the light of a secondhand lamp in the tiny living/dining room of a house I'd rented in the Georgetown area of Washington, D.C. The book in my hand was called *Play It As It Lays.* Written by Joan Didion, it's the story of a beautiful but deeply disturbed woman in Hollywood in the 1960s. The woman, Maria Wyeth, came from a comically small town in Nevada owned totally by her father and mother and a friend. The town was mainly desert, so they were hardly rich, but her father was convinced that he *would* be rich if he simply kept trying, and by trying, he meant gambling.

In one key scene, Maria has returned from her work as a high-fashion model in New York City to visit her mom and dad. Maria announces that she doesn't want to go back to New York. Her mother agrees and says, "She's too thin. Look at her; see for yourself."

Father replies, in a veritable orgy of good sense, "She can't win if she's not at the table."

When I read those words, I was electrified, as if someone had given me a huge shot of Dexedrine. "You can't win if you're not at the table." But of course! You can't win if you're not at the gambling table. And I'd never even gotten near the table in my whole life. Maria Wyeth's father had hit the nail dead-center perfect, right on its head. Getting up to the table is everything.

In my deluded miasma, I had thought that by a miracle of some sort, a messenger of fame would dart into the old *Star* building, take the elevator to the seventh floor, dodge down the lime green passageways past all the children of the secretaries and the dozing lawyers, and enter my office. There he would offer me a lifetime contract as a famous writer—in Hollywood, New York, wherever I chose—at spectacular pay, with all the beautiful girls I could ever want.

But of course, that would never happen, because you can't win if you're not at the table, and there are no messengers of fame except for those standing alongside the tables. If I'd rolled dice in my office for ten years and gotten 10,000 consecutive points, I would never have made a dime. If I'd dealt myself cards for a decade and gotten 5,000 royal flushes, I would never have won a single chip. If I'd bought a little roulette table and rolled my number every time for all eternity, I would never have won a penny. Because the only money you can ever win is paid at the table—and when you're playing in a closed, dim office with no one else there, you're a long way from the table. When you play with yourself—as they say—you don't win a thing.

You can win only when you're at the gaming tables, with other people playing, usually playing against you. You can only win at the tables when there's real, genuine action; real, tangible winning; and real, tangible losing. Only at the place where the action is for our particular wish can we win. If we want to be entrepreneurs, we must go to money-lenders. If we want to be race-car drivers, we must go to the track. If we want to be lovers, we have to go where the boys and girls are. If we want to be great chefs, we have to go to restaurants.

Maria Wyeth could only win as a model at modeling agencies. Her father let her in on that secret. There's a particular table for every want, every heart's desire. You can only win if you're at the table.

If you want to be an actress, you have to try out for parts in two-bit productions where the producer treats you like a piece of meat. If you want to be an architect, you must go to architecture school and then to a firm where the senior people will treat you like an idiot. If you want to own a shop, you must open one and be subject to every kind of abuse from teenage shoplifters. If you want to be an investment banker, you must go to a firm and be prepared to do spreadsheets for two years.

In other words, it hurts to go to the table. But you must go if you're ever to win.

Example: Marti Webb is a celebrated stage actress who appeared in the London production of *Evita* in the starring role. She started acting at the age of 12, but she learned in her early 30s just what it meant to be at the table.

For more than a decade, Marti rolled the dice. She won during her early years, but then faded as the game wore on. She landed major parts in *Oliver!* and *Stop the World—I Want to Get Off* when she was still in her early 20s. Then she had a dry spell. It was painful for her to go to auditions where she was often beaten out for parts by ingenues.

So she stepped away from the table. "I went to work at a travel agency," she said. "It was just too awful going to all those calls and not getting treated decently." She waited for the telephone to ring, for a major producer to call her. The bolt of lightning might come to make her a major Broadway or West End of London star at any moment.

But of course the call did not come. She'd left the table. There was no way that she could possibly win. One day a man came into the travel agency where she was working. He was (and is) a famous English lyricist. "What the hell are you doing here?" he asked. "You should be back at the table."

So Marti went back to the table. She had a hard year, and then came the inevitable: In three months she became the star of *Evita* and recorded an album that put her in the European pop top ten instantly. She'd always possessed the talent. The only lack was the table. No sooner had she returned to it than she made her point.

As always, the only winners—in this case, Marti Webb—were the ones at the table. Yes, it hurts to stay at the table, but that's where life's trophies are awarded.

And they're not always in the form of fame or money.

Arnie, a classmate of mine from law school, didn't dream of being a star. He dreamed of seducing beautiful black-haired girls from Georgetown University. He was obsessed with that goal. He thought of little else every day while working as an economist at the Federal Reserve Board.

Long ago in Washington, D.C., he began his nightly quest for his dream girls by hanging out at Clyde's, a bar that was the "innest" of in places for Georgetown coeds. Sometimes I went to that bar with him, helping him spot his heartthrobs through the trendy indoor plants and English-ale advertisements. Night after night, he would drag himself from his chair, stake out his target girl, and try to strike up a conversation with her. For nine straight nights, the girls looked at him and laughed, or at most let him buy them a drink before sending him on his way.

But Arnie didn't slink back to his tufted and rolled stool at Clyde's with a feeling of defeat. Far from it. He was enjoying the pursuit, even if the chase had not yet led to the catch. For years, he'd watched at a safe distance while the black-haired lovelies of his mind passed by in silent disdain. He'd suffered from terrible tension headaches as he watched hulky college boys effortlessly pick up the nectar and ambrosia of women. Now Arnie was at the table. He was playing the game that could lead to finding his dream girl. And he loved it.

On the tenth evening at Clyde's, he struck up a conversation with an adorable freckle-faced girl named Katie. Then he didn't appear in daylight for three days. When he finally staggered into work on the afternoon of the fourth day, he looked as happy as anyone ever has. He'd finally made his point at the table.

The only way Arnie was ever going to find the Katie he'd always wanted was to go to that table and face repeated rejection. And he learned what *I* had learned and what everyone should learn: It doesn't hurt as much to be at the table as to not be at the table. *It does not hurt to try and fail. What hurts is to fail to try.*

An acquaintance of mine I will call Amador Fuentes told the perfect story of the fresh air of risk. "For years," he said, "I worked as a margin clerk at a brokerage house that specialized in commodities contracts, especially in cotton. Then I worked my way up to handle some accounts for textile factories. And I sometimes walked over to the ring to watch the trading. And I always felt like I could be one of those folks making $3,000 with the turn of a hand because of a particularly sharp trade. But I was in the riskless part of the business, just working off commission for other people. And I was scared to take my own money and trade for my own account. But every day that I saw those kids who were just out of high school making those million-dollar trades, with two points of profit, I just felt sick that I wasn't doing it.

"Finally, after two years, I got my license to trade for my own account. I didn't tell anyone, but I cleared it with my boss. Then I went over to Harry's Bar at the Amex and had a drink. Then I went back and walked into the ring. The next thing I knew, I was yelling and screaming, waving my hands around, just like everybody I'd always wanted to be. I lost $5,000 the first week, but it was the best bargain I ever got for the money. I felt like a king that week just because I'd done it. And I still feel terrific when I realize that I had the balls to do it in the first place."

Amador Fuentes also feels good because he almost never lost money after his first year. He reviews the day's trading every evening from his penthouse on Park Avenue, with a snifter of 1956 Puligny brandy in his hand.

But I hope that you, the reader, don't get the impression that "You can't win if you're not at the table" refers only to types of activities such as writing, picking up dream girls (or dream women), or commodities trading. Stepping up to the table means getting into the arena where you can fight for what you want, even if it takes persistence and determination without even a spin of the roulette wheel.

One of the leading accountants in this country, whom I'll call Joanne, started her career as a schoolteacher in a suburb of Detroit. For several years she taught junior high school children the rudiments of civics. "But it wasn't me," she said. "I learned pretty quickly that I wasn't cut out to hang around with 14-year-olds all day. I wanted to be where the big decisions were being made, the decisions about money."

Joanne had a romantic vision of accountants—a bizarre form of romance to be sure, but that's what makes horse races—and believed that if she could be an accountant, she could sit at the right hand of the gods of commerce. For three years she drove by the campus of the School of Business of the University of Michigan, watching the students go inside. She imagined that they were all learning accountancy, going to the places she wanted to go. But she was afraid that if she gave up teaching, she might not like accounting school either. "I might be caught betwixt and between," she said.

She found out that it was not so. "The first day I walked into accounting class, I can't even remember what it was about. But I remember that I felt great that I was doing what I'd always just imagined doing. I felt so good about myself that I never looked back."

Joanne had experienced the euphoria of taking her first real-world steps toward being what she wanted to be. Even though the table was a quiet one indeed, she had put herself up against the edge of the accountancy table, and that was enough. "Even when I give the CEO of ITT advice about tax planning for their Liberian affiliate, I don't feel as great as I did when I first walked through those doors to accounting school. I felt proud of myself just for trying, and that was what gave me the *oomph* I needed to succeed. I would have killed myself if I still had to teach."

And the euphoria of stepping up to the tables leaves no headache from a morning-after hangover. It's the best kind of "high"—a result of pride in yourself.

❀ ❀ ❀

Let's be realistic. Except in mythology, there are no stories of human beings who step up to the table and make a great fortune on their first roll. Everyone is on the come line (a craps term), and no one makes it right out of the box. Bunkhouse Logic tells us that even the elect of this earth, the most successful people in their fields, simply do not escape the pain of losing initially in their march through life. It's a mileage map on your journey through life, a sign that you've made some progress since you left your cell and ventured out into the world where there are real pleasures and real pains. No, Bunkhouse Logic does not advise masochism, but it does tell you that the pain of striving and failing is experienced just prior to the joy of striving and succeeding—and is an inevitable part of the effort. That effort only matters when it's at the table where you can win.

Don't worry: Being at the table can hurt, but it's also fun. To the true lover of tennis, after all, playing is the thing. Winning will come eventually. But playing is a pleasure in and of itself. To the true student of the law, learning about the topic while practicing is a delight. Later, after he's been at the table for a time, he will, of course, be victorious at most of the trials. But at first, the table itself is a thrill.

The time you put in at the table gives you a certain respectability that you can hardly get in any other way. The other participants actually begin to see you as a fellow player, and they begin to trust you. Then you're inside the door. So enjoy your time at the table. It's inevitable that if you stay there, you'll win in due time. And even when you're losing, you're still making progress.

Michael S., one of the major young producers in Hollywood, explained how success comes in the motion-picture business. "You know," he said, "it's a little talent and a little luck and a little knowing the right person. But I'm absolutely certain at this point that an awful lot of it, most of it, is just staying in Hollywood, working at it. It's longevity, man," he said. "A hell of a lot of success in Hollywood is longevity and nothing else." (See page 84 for Rule of the Game No. 4: *Life Is a Process, and the Process Never Ends.*)

Not just in Hollywood, Michael. The successful of this world know well that they have to stay in the game to win. They know that their time at the table isn't wasted. They expect that they'll have to spend a lot of time at the table before they can begin to win. They expect that they'll have to develop a reputation. Only the failures think that they'll win the first time and every time. They're the ones who get discouraged and take their marbles and go home. It never enters the mind of the naturally successful that they'll be instant celebrities. They roll away steadily at the craps table through the night, and in time, they win all they ever wanted.

Again, think of the cowboy. Think of activity and inner mobility. The cowboy wants to learn to be a bull rider. He wants to be able to throw himself up onto that Brahmin bull and stay on. If he does, he's a lead-pipe cinch to get the prettiest girl at the Paragon Bar in Aspen, Colorado, even if her last name is Hilton.

So he begins to learn to ride the bull, and he hardly even gets aboard the first few times. He expects no less. He has the inner mobility to know that he's learning. He barely gets on before he's thrown off the next dozen times, but it doesn't bother him. He has the activity to know that he must stay at the table of bull riding even if he does get thrown a few times.

Step up to that table. You know, it's the only place where they pass out the goodies of life. Stay at that table. Have a good time there. Enjoy the game while you wait for the rewards to come your way.

The irrefutable truth is this: *You cannot win if you're not at the table.* But you can win if you stay at the table—and if you know the rules.

〰 〰 〰

PART V

THE RULES OF THE GAME

You've decided what you want. You've asked for what you want. And you've realized that you can't win if you're not at the table. Now you've stepped up to the table, and it's time for you to learn the Rules of the Game.

Only an idiot plays a game without knowing the rules. The successful people of this world only play the games whose rules they know. You wouldn't expect to get on a tennis court without knowing how to play by the rules and then win. You would never go to a poker game totally ignorant of the rules and expect to come out ahead. You would never in a million years dream of going to a craps table without any idea of what the come line is and still expect to win.

By the same token, in the game of getting what you want out of life—and thereby restoring self-esteem—you must also know exactly how the game is played. Luckily, those who are truly successful have left behind a complete manual of instructions as to how to play and win.

The rules aren't detailed models of every conceivable game. There are far too many subgames in life for any one book to tell you the rules of every single possibility. But I can do something even better for you: I can tell you the rules for the one game that matters, the one that controls all the others: *getting what you want from life.*

Bunkhouse Logic lays out the rules that you must apply to yourself to win that game. The rules of this game aren't such things as "Collect $200 when you pass Go." Those are trivial rules that you can pick up in an hour. The rules that really control who wins and who loses are rules of the mind—patterns of thought, behavior, attitude, and expectation—which make all the difference in everything you do, no matter what the particular instruction manual may say.

Remember that Bunkhouse Logic tells you that when you ask for what you want, the key person to ask is *yourself.* In understanding the Rules of the Game, you are once again the key. It doesn't matter if anyone else in your circle or family or business knows the Rules of the Game, explicitly or implicitly. As long as *you* know them, you will triumph.

※ ※ ※

Rule of the Game No. 1:
Concentrate on "How to"; Forget "Why Not"

Don't Fence Yourself In

One of the greatest American success stories involves Herbert Hoover. In 1893 he went to Northern California to become a prospector and speculator. "The Panic of 1893 was raging in the East," Hoover later said, "and everyone there was going broke. But I didn't know a thing about it. So I came west and made my fortune. I was a millionaire many times over before I learned that what I had done was impossible."

Hoover's story was and is a perfect example of what the human spirit can do when it's not hobbled by artificial restraints. You can achieve your heart's desire by repeated effort, imagination, inner mobility, activity, and the application of Bunkhouse Logic. But you cannot do it if you tell yourself that it's impossible. You cannot do it if you lock yourself in your own prison of thought.

Has this ever happened to you? You're lying on your bed on a Sunday afternoon, reading the newspaper. You pick up the news section and read about someone exactly your age, without any special hereditary background, without any particular skills, without having been touched on the shoulder by an angel of the Lord. Yet that person is doing exactly what you've always wanted to do. He's a successful commodities broker or a renowned artist or has the most perfectly behaved children—all superb scholars—that you could ever imagine.

But wait a minute. Just hold on. *Why can't I become that person in the newspaper?* That is just what you ask yourself. *I'm just as able (or talented or good-looking) as that person. What happened?*

You lie on your bed, staring at the afternoon football game, explaining why you can't get the things you want: "My mother was mean to me." "I always played on the bench in high school basketball." "My nose is too long." "I was the wrong religion." "I didn't go to boarding school." "I don't have the right kind of car." "My father is a drunk." Before long, you have a incredibly supportive list of all the reasons why you're not getting the things you want out of life. Now you can enjoy the third and fourth quarters of the football game on TV without any psychic interruptions.

Forget it. That's exactly the way to prolong your failure, the perfect way to ensure that your feelings of inadequacy and self-loathing persist throughout all history. If you dredge up a lot of excuses for not doing anything, then you will surely *not* do anything. And then, when you pick up the newspaper next Sunday and read about the newest man or woman who's doing exactly what you want to do, you'll ensure that you feel even worse than you did the weekend before. Don't do it. Let yourself out of the "Why not?" jail.

Bunkhouse Logic suggests that if you consider the following proposition, you'll unquestionably find that it's true: Within the limits of mortality, you can do what you think you *can* do . . . and you *cannot* do what you think you cannot do. Once again, the key thoughts are your own.

Every moment that you spend collecting excuses is time wasted. Every reason you make up for why you haven't accomplished the things you want to is a nail in the coffin of your self-respect over the long run. Yes, in the short run, it's great comfort to realize that the reason your college roommate is rich and you're poor is that he has blond hair and you don't. Also, just as surely, you would be a lot happier if you went out and made yourself rich instead of making up an excuse for why you're so far from what you want.

If an army burns its bridges behind it, the soldiers' mouths will likely go dry from fear. But by the same token, they'll have a powerful incentive to succeed. If you tell yourself that you're only giving yourself points for success, you give yourself a similar incentive.

This particular rule—*Concentrate on "how to"; forget "why not"*—requires shedding the habits of a lifetime. Almost all of us have been brought up with great acquired skills in rationalizing. We're all far more adept at planning the rationalizations of failure than in planning how to succeed. It's all a waste of time.

But, again, imagine yourself as a cowboy, tending a large herd of cattle. Your map tells you that you have 100 miles to go to get the cattle to market. If you don't get the cattle to market, all is lost. No rationalization, however appealing to a Freudian, will help. You simply have to get the job done. So you do it.

That is just how Bunkhouse Logic suggests you view your life. It's a drive to the place where you get your rewards (in a sense it's also a drive to where you get your Final Reward). If you don't reach your destination, you can make every excuse in the book. Your wife or your husband and your friends will cluck sympathetically. But underneath, you will know, and they will know, that you've failed. That's true whether your goal is money or power, the lover of your dreams, or praise from your family about your great cooking.

This may sound severe, but it actually is not. The real cruelty would be to allow yourself to avoid success year after year by letting yourself get locked into a negative-thinking, "Why not?" frame of mind. Don't do it. Avoid getting addicted to all the reasons and excuses why you can't succeed. If you take all that time and instead apply it to trying out all the techniques of success, you'll soon be successful.

So set yourself free. Go out and get what you want—without having one leg in a shackle of self-made promises to fail.

Example: Suppose you want—more than anything—to go off to Aruba with that beautiful woman in the publicity department. She's a long-legged, snooty-looking creature who went to Vassar, but you love the way she lisps. You can just picture her lying next to you in a little grass shack, with the surf pounding the beach outside.

But you tell yourself over and over again that you can't even ask her to lunch because, after all, you're just a little creep from City College. You tell yourself that she must hang out exclusively with heirs and magnates, and that she'd spit on you if you came near her. So you stay away and are gnawed by anxiety and loss.

If you spend your time finding out what she likes so that you could make her fall in love with you, you might be on that first mile to Aruba. You might just pass by her desk and start talking about restaurants. When you find out which one is her favorite, then you could wait a few days and ask her out. You could find out what movies she likes. You could find out what she likes to do on a Sunday afternoon. You could find out what her politics are, or how she feels about the national energy policy or strategic arms limitation.

Then there would be a patch of common ground on which you could communicate. Then you might be two miles toward Aruba. You would have started the process of getting her to be your friend, instead of telling yourself over and over how impossible it might be.

Think about it: NASA put a man on the moon in an unheard-of amount of time. But there were moments when a certain part of the effort looked impossible. However, it was simply not acceptable for anyone to verbalize the fact that this magnificent goal wasn't attainable. So, while engineers and scientists worked on the seemingly insoluble problem, other scientists and engineers raced forward with the rest of the rocket. The state of mind of the space program was that if you were convinced that *anything* was possible, then the only question was "How?" As you know, that was the greatest scientific and manufacturing effort in history, culminating in brilliant success.

The anxiety and energy that might have surrounded the ultimate question of "Why not?" was converted into momentum about "How to." That energy—a considerable force—got the job done. That's how it should be in the lives of all individuals. You must get rid of the notion that there's any reward at all for the interesting excuses. Only your mommy or your high school teacher might consider your excuses amusing. No one else will. Least of all will *you* consider your excuses fascinating after you've told them to yourself over and over again.

Disregard Negative Advice

A certain man in New York told me this story:

"I was a trial lawyer," he said, "working my ass off on really hard cases. In return for that, I got tiny little amounts of money that barely paid my bills. I saw that the people I worked for were making really substantial money in tax shelters.

"They'd pull up at my office in limousines while I got ready to go home on the subway. So I figured that tax shelters were a pretty good way to make money. So I studied the law, and I figured out one that sounded pretty good.

"I went to all these guys I worked for, and I told them the scam. They looked at me and then at each other and then said, 'It's an interesting concept, but it can't work.' They gave me about 20 reasons why it would be impossible to put the deal together. Then they went to The Four Seasons in their limos.

"I told myself that I was going to be more successful than all of them put together in a year. I didn't care how impossible it was to put it together. If it was legal, I'd get it done." The narrator of this tale stopped for a moment to ring a silver bell, which called his chef.

"I'd see the people in their suits from Paul Stuart, and I knew that I wanted the same things. So I went on the road, talking to every rich person I had ever heard of to ask them if they had an income-tax problem. If someone said he did, I told him I had a way to save some of that tax for him. Now, most of the people I talked to wouldn't give me the time of day. They said the scheme sounded harebrained, and they had always used so-and-so for tax shelters, and they weren't buying. But a few said yes. And I went all over the place and got a few more people in Salt Lake and places the old-line shelter people wouldn't bother going to.

"And some rancher in Utah would tell a surgeon in Ogden about me, and he'd tell a guy who owned a department store, and pretty soon, I had enough people. Then I had it half done, and still, all the people back in New York were telling me it couldn't be done. I told them to screw off. Not only could it be done, but it *would* be done.

"I'd get so wrapped up in it that sometimes I'd drive off the road. Once I twisted the gearshift lever on my Datsun right off because I was grabbing it while I was concentrating. But in a year, I got it done. And in that year, from start to finish, I made almost $40 million. For me. Personally. No one had ever dreamed that there was that much money in tax shelters. In that one year, I became the General Motors of tax shelters. Then I quit."

The man told me this story in the dining room of his palatial mansion in Bel Air. He's been offered millions for his house, and he won't sell. "I use it as a pied-à-terre when I'm in L.A.," he said.

This story of Michael W., the king of tax shelters, is not really about tax shelters at all. It's entirely about how the world will always tell you that your idea is no good, that you're a fool to pursue it, that many people have tried before and failed, and hey, if it's such a good idea, why hasn't it been done before? The world around you and me is filled to the very brim with naysayers. Bunkhouse Logic assures you that they are wrong.

As we all know, the nature of people is to be pessimistic and dour about anything out of the ordinary. Most people are stuck in their own little ruts, their same jobs, their same houses, their same families, and their same two-inch horizons. If you waltz in one day with a plan for how you're going to have a Bentley and a house in Bel Air in one year, those people in a rut will be scared. It might really happen! You, who once were a schlemiel just like them, might really and truly be a multimillionaire in a year if you go forward with your scheme.

Naturally, your success would just accentuate the other guy's failure. He must therefore discourage you from even attempting a venture that might humiliate him so thoroughly. That's where his pessimism and his naysaying come from. It is in no sense a reasonable criticism of your plan. That sneering is just your neighbor's way of hindering you from thoroughly showing him up. Don't fall into his trap and let yourself be sidetracked from your goal!

Even when the criticism isn't personally motivated by jealousy, it's usually based on less information than you have. Much more important, it's an opinion issued by someone with no stake in the outcome of the scheme—except a desire for it to fail. You, on the other hand, know that you can put your matchless energy and perseverance into the dubious equation. That human factor—you and what you can do—will make all the difference.

Bunkhouse Logic tells you that when the next fellow over in the car pool tells you that it's simply impossible to market "love oil" made from mineral oil and inexpensive artificial fragrances (or else why wouldn't Colgate do it?), he speaks from jealousy, ignorance, and being out of touch. The several millionaires in this country marketing those "love oils," however smarmy their customers, faced and overcame just such negative thinking. And it's a lot more reputable than Enron.

Bunkhouse Logic cheers you on by saying that if the man across from you at the dinner table laughs lightly and says that it's a nice dream for you to think of being the first woman CEO at JPMorgan Chase, he cannot see into your heart and know just how determined you are that the dream become a reality. If he had an inkling of just how set you were on your presidency, he would go to Vegas and bet that you would make it into the executive washroom.

The primary harm in negative advice is that it prevents too many fine people like you from doing the key work in getting your heart's desire: planning how you're going to get it. Discouragement from others keeps you from ever going into the map room of your mind and digging out the precise coordinates of the journey from the bleak present to the golden future.

It is just those maps that are the key. As difficult as the trip may seem to you, there's almost always a way to get there. Your friends and co-workers will tell you that there's no way to get there from here. But they're dead wrong. You are sitting on the BMT, heading in from Ocean Avenue in Brooklyn to Manhattan, thumbing through *Vogue,* looking at the rich and famous. And you think, *Holy cow! I don't want to work in the back room of New York Life Insurance Company all my life. I want to be a powerful fashion designer like Donna Karan.* And the girl next to you, who went through Erasmus Hall High School with you, says, "Forget it! There's no way you can ever do it. You're stuck in the back room for life."

Not at all, not at all. Somewhere there's a map of how it can be done. And if you let your friend block the door to the map room, then you're a fool. Your friend has her own reasons for not wanting you to ever come close to being Donna Karan. Her advice is her reality, not yours, so don't worry about her. First worry about how you'll pay for design school, and then where you'll work after graduating, and what your specialty will be. Worry about the "How to" of getting where you want. The techniques involved in moving toward your goal are what will take you where you want to be. Let your friend Shirley, back on the D train, tell her other friends the story of how LaVerne, her old pal from high school, who used to ride this same rotten train, is that woman in the picture on page 292 of *Vogue,* in the feature "New Summer Fashions for You." Let Shirley brag about you while she's still in her rut. You'll get out of it by concentrating on the mechanics of going where you need to go and forgetting about why it's impossible.

Chuck Yeager, America's most famous test pilot, broke the sound barrier in 1947. He was the first human being to do so. He was a poor country boy from the hollows of West Virginia, from a place "so dark they had to pipe in sunlight." He knew little about engineering or physics. So while the physicists and engineers studied the theories of sonic waves, he flew airplanes by the seat of his pants. And when the first pilots died trying to crack the sound barrier, the physicists and engineers said that this barrier was like a concrete wall—it simply couldn't be penetrated. But Yeager knew how to fly from here to there and actually lived a great period of his life right next to the speed of sound. One day while the academicians were teaching students that the sound barrier could never be broken, Yeager just opened up the throttle on his rocket plane a little wider and passed the sound barrier without a bump.

Yeager had been in the sky long enough to know that a thing like a concrete wall in the sky simply could not exist. He completely ignored the negative advice of those who were in ivory towers. He forgot about "Why not?" and concentrated on "How to." In his case, "How to" was just pushing the rocket plane a little bit farther. Chuck Yeager knew the "How to" of flying, just as each one of you has to learn the "How to" of getting wherever you want to get . . . and unlearn the "Why nots?" that have been thrown at you all your life.

Seek Out Those Who Know How to Get It Done

The youth of America get out of school knowing why Giotto is the direct antecedent of Picasso, or they used to, but once they're out in the real world, they have no idea how to get the things they want out of life—financially, creatively, romantically, or any other way. The cowboy, whose education has been spent accomplishing things and getting things done, has a far better foundation for getting his heart's desire than the student who got an A for her senior thesis on why the League of Nations failed. The successful in this world, those who bet on themselves and win, have had to learn on their own just how to move from square A to square B and on to the winning position. They didn't get those secrets of activity and inner mobility in school.

You've been obliged all your life to learn how to criticize—how to apply "Why not?" to your own life. Now you'll have to forget that school for failure and learn "How to," just as the winners of the world have. And you'll have to learn it from these very people. Brace yourself and dive off that lofty plane where intellectuals explain why everything is impossible. Get into the soup where plumbers learn how to fix boilers, farmers learn how to plant corn, financial vice presidents learn how to float bond issues, politicians know how to get along with the people who can make their careers, and decorators learn how to dress like winners. Take all you can from their knowledge and their realization that it can be done. Let their success validate your reality.

A man I'll call Bob Schiller, one of the major players in the worldwide grain market who operates out of Duluth, Minnesota, explained to me the necessary corollary of this refusal to acknowledge negative thinking. "If you meet somebody who knows how to get up the greasy pyramid, and that person is willing to show you how it's done, stay very close to that same person."

Schiller's point is well taken. There are so few people who will encourage you and tell you that your dreams are possible that when you find one, you should and must listen to him and cleave to him. If, on top of that, the positive thinker knows how to get it done, he is the person of your dreams.

"When I started out in grain," Schiller said, "I was an economist for Cargill. I'd just gotten out of the University of Minnesota and I thought I knew all there was to know about grain. But after a year or two, I realized that I was just a clerk writing numbers on pieces of graph paper for $190 a week. If I disappeared the next day, no one would even notice for a month.

"The guys who really counted were the traders, those boys down on the floor of the exchange who wheeled and dealed with the real money—not the abstractions I worked with—10,000 bushels at a clip. They were the ones who actually set the price. Plus, they were the ones who actually made the money. They wouldn't have thought my salary was worth mentioning. So I decided I was going to be a trader. Not just a trader for Cargill, but an independent trader, making real money for myself.

"One time when I was in New York at India House, I started talking to a man who happened to work for the commodities department of Eastman, Dillon. He told me he thought it could be done. 'There's a lot of guys making a half million a year who are a lot stupider than you,' he said.

"He told me how to start getting the money together to do a little trading through his company. It was much easier than I thought. Then he showed me how I could buy a correspondent seat with another broker and save most of my commissions. He said he'd bet that with what I knew about crop forecasting, he could find some people to back me up in getting my own seat on the Chicago exchange.

"That was the hard part—getting people to part with their money. But I talked to a lot of people, and a few were interested. So I got them to give me a little money—as an investment, and not a loan. That was when Cargill heard about it and fired me. But by then I had a good head of steam up. I started trading for myself the next month. I was scared as hell. The first day I was tired because I couldn't sleep at all the night before. But I learned how to get those trades made, and I had a good idea that the Russians were going to be in the market pretty heavily. So I bought long— a lot. And at the end of the first week, I was way ahead of the game.

"The thing is, it's been 11 years now, and I still see the old gang I used to work with in Cargill's forecasting department. I'm not any smarter than they are. I just had this lucky break to meet a man who got me off brooding about how stuck I was, and showed me I wasn't stuck at all. That guy I met at India House made me realize that all I had to think about was how to get it done, instead of worrying about whether I could do it or not."

Remember, Bunkhouse Logic assures you that there are few people who indeed can and will bother to help you with both encouragement and advice on the practical side. When you meet one, do not even hesitate for a moment. That is the person you want to be around. Forget the people who tell you it can't be done.

If You Thought It Was Bad Before

Once you've begun to succeed, you'll notice an interesting facet of human nature. Your "friends" will shower you with more negative comments in direct proportion to how successful you've become. If you're a salesman, they'll tell you that you can't be sales manager. When you become sales manager, they'll tell you that you can't be vice president of sales. When you're vice president, they'll swear that no sales veep has ever made it to president. And then when you become president, they'll stop speaking to you, pure and simple.

This is called jealousy. It's one of the most powerful of human emotions. It grows in tenacity as you grow more worthy of envy. Expect it to come up constantly. This isn't your particular cross to bear. This is simply life unfolding. Don't let it throw you off your trail any more than the cowboy lets one little thunderstorm throw him off *his* trail. Enough said.

※ ※ ※

Rule of the Game No. 2:
Notice What Is, Not What Should Be

The Rules of Life Are Learned from Experience and Not from Logic

Of all the sticking points that can hold you back once you're on the move from your own room 710 of the spirit—that deadly place where I was stuck before I rebelled and claimed my own destiny—to the place you want to be, the most unyielding can be false expectations from the world—the tenacious belief that there's any relation at all between what is and what should be, between the actual and the just, can be paralyzing.

On a daily basis, every one of us is subjected to almost as many volts as it takes to light up Las Vegas. The electricity comes in the form of continual shocks of realization that there's an infinitude of discrepancy between what happens every day and what should happen . . . if there were any moral order in the world. The repeated excruciating blows of seeing the least deserving kid get the most, of seeing the poor made poorer, of seeing them that have getting even more—all of that can make a sane person go back into his room, get into bed, pull up the covers, and never come out.

Don't let it happen to you. Instead of wasting your time crying about how illogical life is, just accept it. Life is incredibly illogical. It bears no relation to justice or logic or romantic notions. It just rolls along, like Ol' Man River. You will have no more success getting life to reshape itself into a logical or just form than you would have trying to move the Mississippi River to Africa.

If you spend your life trying to reconcile life with logic, yours will be a wasted life. If you accept life as it is, you will be a country mile down the road to success.

Of course, there's a lot of pain in giving up the notion of an orderly, just universe. It's like abandoning belief in the tooth fairy or in Peter Pan. The world is a grimmer place—at first—without that belief. It looks dark and random. But when you accept the reality principle—in this case, that life does not work off a logical schematic—you lose a lot of vulnerability to fate.

Yes, it is frightening to think that life goes by the rule of "What will be, will be." But it takes an enormous load off your back if you finally accept it.

There Is No Heavenly Mandate That Things Will Work Out as They Should

If you get that rule in the depths of your bones, you will start to be able to cope. You'll begin to see that the world runs on chaotic, strange lines, which cannot readily be predicted.

In addition, your idea of "should" is almost always highly colored by wishing—to put it mildly. You see that events should logically work out to a certain conclusion. But in your equation, there are bound to be variables that you've called constants, and vice versa. There's bound to be a certain amount of egocentricity in all your calculations of unselfish impartiality.

That is all well and good and perfectly normal. It means, however, that your idea of what should be a logical or fair outcome may appear neither fair nor logical to anyone else. (So just forget about "should" as a way of forecasting events.)

If you're free of the superstition of expecting the world to run like your idea of logic, you're free indeed. Instead of holing up in your attic nursing your wounds because you didn't get sent on that boondoggle to Los Angeles, you will see what led the boss to select old Higginbotham instead. Freed of your crippling innocence about logic, you will not sulk endlessly when you see that everyone in your law-school class is making more money than you are. Instead, you will investigate reality and find out what they're doing that has put them where you should be.

True freedom is thoroughly intermixed with the reality principle. To see life as it is, is a great blessing indeed. "Freedom tastes of reality," as The Who said.

The cowboy who heads out into the plains to guide his cattle to market should not expect to run into more than one rattlesnake on a whole trip. But if he does run into more than one snake, he doesn't go back to his pickup, roll up the windows, and sulk. He just goes back to the second snake or the third snake or the fourth snake, and he shoots them, one by one. Activity and inner mobility.

If the cowboy heading across Wyoming from Sheridan to Jackson comes across three dry holes in a row, he doesn't say, "This is impossible. I'm not supposed to run across any more than one dry hole, tops, on this trip. I'm quitting. I'm going home to Mother." He just changes his direction until he finds some holes that aren't dry. Learn from him.

Driving with Your Eyes Open

Deanne Barkley is one smart cookie. For many years she was the most powerful woman in network television broadcasting. As a vice president of NBC, she was responsible for such knockout hits as *Holocaust* and *Little House on the Prairie.* Now she's a happily retired woman in Hawaii. She has a saying about life: "It's a freeway." She adds, "If you simply know your destination, you will eventually get where you want to be."

That's the whole point behind Bunkhouse Logic's first rule: *Decide what you want.*

But there's an addendum: You can drive anywhere you want to go if your eyes are open and on the road. If your eyes are closed, you can't get out of the driveway. Imagine trying to drive across the Verrazano-Narrows Bridge with your eyes closed. You'd be in the water before you turned off the radio.

In the great adventure of life, your eyes are closed if you concentrate on what *should* be instead of what is. You simply miss the traffic, the cars coming toward you, the stoplights, the bends—everything that's on the road if you don't bear down on what *is* instead of what should be. You couldn't drive while keeping your eyes closed and dreaming of a Tahitian sunset. It's just as impossible to progress through life alive and well if you don't look at the world around you.

You may very well say, "Oh, but life is so grim. I won't think about the way it is. I'll just think about the way it should be. I won't think about the cruel, unpredictable publicity departments and vengeful, cantankerous bosses. Instead, I'll think about Trump Tower and ball gowns." You can do that, but it's just as dangerous as saying, "Oh, I hate all those billboards and auto graveyards along the side of the highway. I think I'll bring along a television and just watch as I drive." In both cases, you're begging to get smashed up.

On the other hand, once you start driving by looking at the road and seeing which cars to avoid and which signs to follow, you're en route to real progress. You can drive. You can make your way to your destination. You can see just what it takes to get to Washington, D.C., from New York City along the New Jersey Turnpike if you keep your eyes open. And you can see just how to get the job you've always dreamed of. You can avoid the accidents—in cars and in life—that keep you from reaching nirvana.

Driving with your eyes open also lets you see that it's really not as hard as you thought it was when you had your eyes closed. The clincher is that with your eyes open, you can get somewhere. With your eyes closed, you're heading for an early demise—either while still living or by dying.

None of this means that you should give up your fantasies of what life is or should be in terms of your goals. Bunkhouse Logic insists that you keep close hold of your most sensational dreams—to be the star of a Broadway musical, to be the head of a billion-dollar company, to be the spouse of a kind and spiritual person.

Keep your most dreamlike goals. But go about getting them realistically, not blinded by fantastic illusions of how life *should* be.

The cowboy roaming across the plains doesn't close his eyes and fantasize that he's in a bar in Laramie just because the rain begins to fall. He knows that if he *does* close his eyes, he's likely to lose his horse in a marmot hole. The cowboy heading across the badlands doesn't close his eyes and imagine that he's with the cute go-go dancer in Montrose just because one of his cattle is bitten by a gopher. He just keeps his eyes open a little wider for gophers.

That's exactly the way you must be in the office towers of Manhattan, on the back lots of Burbank, in the shopping centers of Oak Park, in the countinghouses of New Orleans, in the refineries of Odessa, in the real-estate offices of Phoenix, in the paper mills of Seattle, and in the antique shops of San Francisco.

With your eyes open, you'll achieve the things that give you the pride in yourself that you want and need for happiness. Eyes closed—forget about it.

Bitter Medicine, but It Works

The Arabs, a people inured to privation and harshness, say, "The blow that does not break my back makes me stronger." So true, so true. The blows of life that rain down upon each and every one of us can either break your back or make you stronger. Bunkhouse Logic tells you that your only choice—a true Hobson's choice—is to endure the blows that make you stronger by letting you realize that this is the way life really is.

It hurts to acknowledge that life is as arduous as it is, but that acknowledgment will help you over many a rough period in the long run. Further, it is fundamental knowledge to the successful of the world. They take for granted that the world is a tough place. So should you. It's part of accepting reality.

A famous economist—my father, in fact—happened to have worked as an advisor to a certain President of the United States. That President left office, and so did his advisor. The President went off to lecture and play golf. The economist went off to teach at a university. Lo and behold, one day the former President came to spend a week at the university. Festivities were organized and took place. As it happened, the economist was the only person at the university who actually knew the former President. The former advisor was not invited to any of the festivities for the former President. Not any of them.

"A few years ago," the economist said, "this would have really blown my brains out. I would have been so agitated that I could have hardly slept. I would have paced back and forth and thought of quitting. And I would have sulked for a month. But I have finally learned enough to let go of all of that.

"That's the key: letting go of all your illusions that anything will work out in a just or decent or proper way. When the President came down here this time, I just knew that however it could have been worked out so that it was most insulting to me, that's how it would work out. So I wasn't surprised when it went off the way it did. It would have hurt if I expected anything else. But I didn't. And it didn't."

The economist, a natural Bunkhouse Logician, added: "The whole thing is just the way life works. It doesn't tell me to be passive, and I wouldn't be passive in any event. It does tell me that if I want satisfaction in life, it will certainly not come from the powers that be at this university. It will come from my own exertions, pure and simple."

Well put, Professor Dad. Of course, but *bien sûr*, the people who run the university will not give you the time of day. That is the nature of university life. There's no sense in pouting about it. The only sense is to take account of it—eyes open—and go on about your business.

When you go to a clothing company to sell your designs, the junior buyer will spend most of the interview talking on the telephone to her friend about their weekend in Southampton. Don't be the slightest bit surprised. Of course she'll call you Renée when your name is Ronnie. Don't expect anything else. That's just the way life goes. It's the equivalent of the poisoned water hole for the cowboy. You can't go home and sulk about it any more than the cowboy can just pack up and quit in the middle of the cattle drive. Instead, you learn just what the buyer is interested in, and you say, "And not only that, but my look is perfect for Southampton." Then you're beginning to learn just exactly what it means to notice what *is* and not what should be.

The cowboy, the Bunkhouse Logician, uses his perceptions of life's cruelties as the stepping-off points for his movements toward success. You can do it, too.

❊ ❊ ❊

Rule of the Game No. 3:
Luck Is Catching

Everybody Needs Luck

Suetonius, the great Roman historian, wrote a series of histories about the debauchery and craziness of the latter days of the Roman empire. The Romans, he said, began to see their era being played out by about the year A.D. 200. Each emperor was worse than the one before, and each day brought new reports of catastrophes in Germany and Scythia. The soothsayers were at work constantly trying to find out what had gone wrong. They came to the conclusion— after a long convention at the Brundisium Hyatt House— that the emperors were unlucky. The cure, they said, was for Rome to find its luckiest citizens and move them into the emperor's palace. Their luck would be absorbed into the emperor's atmosphere and he would breathe it in along with everything else he inhaled. Then he would become lucky and the empire would be saved.

Unfortunately, the next emperor, Julian, was extremely scientific. He found the soothsayers' recommendations preposterous and didn't pursue them. A few months after he assumed the throne, he marched at the head of a huge legion into Persia. The campaign was going swimmingly until a group of Persian harriers galloped down from the hills and flung a few spears at the column. As it happened, one of those spears struck no one but Julian himself and penetrated his leather armor. It lodged in his liver and killed him that night. His troops became so dispirited that they were routed by the Persians. The Roman generals signed a treaty of adhesion with the Persians, and that was the beginning of the end of the Roman Empire.

Julian didn't realize a basic fact of human life: Luck, like measles and the chicken pox, is catching. Good luck can be caught by hanging around with lucky people. And bad luck can be caught by associating with unlucky people. The obvious conclusion: Associate only with lucky people.

The Rational View

There are two ways to look at this phenomenon of luck's contagiousness. First, you might say that luck only appears to be catching. Really and in fact, a far deeper mechanism is at work. Lucky people, so this theory would have you believe, are competent people. Lucky people are hardworking people. Lucky people are well-prepared people. They're not really lucky, so this scheme would say. They only seem to be lucky because of their competence, their diligence, and their preparedness.

Additionally, or so this concept goes, lucky people are usually confident people, sure of themselves because of upbringing or because of a history of success. So once again they give the appearance of being confident of their luck, when they are just plain confident, period.

We all know of examples of just how true this is. The man who just happened to run into the chairman of the board on his summer vacation and came back to find that he was vice president of development now has an air of confidence and invincibility about him. The woman who happened to go to school with the daughter of the largest stockholder of a major publishing company and now has her own imprint at the same company looks not only lucky but also knowledgeable and capable.

So the rational view would say: The same breaks happen to everyone, but certain people know how to take advantage of them better than others.

Whether that view is true or not doesn't really matter. Whether luck is simply a term used to describe certain not-at-all-chancy phenomena or not, certain people definitely have it, and certain people do not. Those who have it possess an aura of calm, confident certainty about themselves. The whole process is circular, though, because as they protect this image of calm, confident certainty, they become more and more likely to get the good things they want out of life. Thus they appear to be luckier and luckier.

You want to spend your time with those people. As a matter of human nature, we imitate the people we're with. This happens quite automatically, without any conscious effort whatsoever. If we're unconsciously modeling ourselves on calm, confident people, we'll start to become winners ourselves. (See the earlier material on the importance of role models in determining what we want from life and asking for it.) If we spend a lot of time around people who get things done, we will become doers and go-getters ourselves. If we go into the jungle of the successful of the world, we'll start to change our coloration—like chameleons—until we look like successful people ourselves.

Ken, an executive of a major semiconductor company, told of his experience in moving from a regional office of Burroughs (now Unisys) to a headquarters office. "I'd been out in this regional quagmire in Columbus, Ohio, trying desperately to understand how the whole software business worked. The offices were in a slummy neighborhood not far from the university. The people were mostly old hacks who never got anything done from one month to the next. They were shabby. They had ketchup stains on ties from Tie City. I began to be just like them.

"The thing was, I was smart enough to realize that I was getting to be like them. They never got anywhere, and I wasn't getting anywhere. So I decided that I needed out. I wrote a letter to the head of Burroughs, telling him that even though I was 35, I wanted to come to Danbury for the training program in the executive offices. They let me.

"I was in shock the very first minute I walked in the door. Everyone looked like an ad for Brooks Brothers. The executives were all neat and well dressed. They spoke in carefully modulated tones. They got all their work done every day. Things always seemed to break their way.

"When I first got there, I thought, *Jesus, these are the luckiest people in the world. They get every card. I'll never be like them.* But I was wrong. I hadn't been there more than a couple of weeks before I started to feel like everything was going my way. I could see myself looking better in the mirror. And I knew I was getting a lot more work done. And then little things started happening to me, like getting sent on really good trips. I started to feel like I was getting the breaks."

Ken left Burroughs and went to a small computer-terminal company. "There I was, and I still had my old habits from Burroughs, and everybody just thought I was the hottest thing on wheels. They thought I was as lucky as the Aga Khan. So I associated only with the head of the company, who was a really put-together guy, and I started getting even more breaks. Pretty soon, a headhunter came and asked me to go to National Semiconductor, and from there

I came here. And I just kept hanging around with the top dogs everywhere I went, and I just felt luckier and luckier."

Ken's story is simply the crystallization of the experience that we've all had. When we spend time with lucky, successful people, we feel lucky and successful ourselves. We even start *acting* lucky and successful ourselves. Something about that luck rubs off.

"I would rather have a lucky general than a smart general in any battle," said Napoleon, who should have known. "They win battles and they make me lucky."

The rational view is that people who, by reason of their superior training, readiness, and ability, give the impression of being lucky lead you into habits of competence that make *you* look lucky. That is more than adequate reason to pass as much time as possible with people who are lucky. You know the feeling: Lunch at any place at all with a genuinely lucky person and you walk out of that restaurant feeling like you're floating on a cloud. If you could turn that one lunch into most of the day, for all the days to come, you'd start getting a lot more done—and you'd feel luckier. It's definitely catching. To win at the great games of life, you need luck. You're either born with it or you can catch it. Bunkhouse Logic tells you to catch it as you can.

The Typhoid Marys of Bad Luck—Stay Away

If the rational explanation of luck and its contagion makes sense for lucky people, it adds up in spades for unlucky people. Bad luck is more readily catching than measles or the summer cold.

Everyone knows how it works. Into your life comes someone who is pitiful because of his bad luck. He keeps denting his old Ford Escort. He lent money to a friend who ran off to Barbados. He lost his wife to a bass player in Mendocino. He can't keep a job.

He seems so helpless and sad that you just want to help him all you can. You make a point of taking him to Burger King for lunch when no one else wants to come near him. You lend him your Camry when his car is in the shop. You ask him to come over and watch *Everybody Loves Raymond* with you while he's all alone. And you extend a ton and a half of sympathy to the poor schlemiel. Gradually, you find yourself spending most of your spare time with this unlucky man.

A funny thing begins to happen. Your friend, "el unluckyo," does not get any luckier. But you start to get markedly more unlucky.

You start to trip just walking down the sidewalk. You smack that Camry into a wall in your parking lot. You get ketchup on the front of your new suit at Burger King. When you fiddle with the television to get Raymond's flesh tones a little clearer, the television breaks.

Not only that, but at work you start to draw the assignments that you know lead nowhere. You and your boss suddenly have nothing to talk about anymore. When he takes the guys out to lunch at the local steak house, you aren't invited. When you go to make your sales calls, your customers aren't there. When they are there, they've just ordered their year's supply of widgets from that new Taiwanese widget distributor.

There's no doubt about it. You start to get unlucky. Your luck changes. As if the unlucky man were a chimney sweep covered in soot, that soot starts to rub off on you. As if the unlucky fellow were carrying typhoid and you happened to share a bowl of soup with him, you start to get sick. Bad luck is catching.

The rational explanation of this makes perfect sense. There are really no such people as unlucky people, this explanation goes. There are just ordinary people who are unprepared for what happens to them. In the struggle for existence, these people have somehow missed the boat. They're not confident. They lack competence. They're not knowledgeable where they should be knowledgeable. They haven't learned the social graces. Whatever it takes to make a go of life in the 21st century, they don't have it.

If these people—perceived as unlucky—had the discipline, the motivation, or the character to make something happen in their lives, they'd stop being so unlucky. If an unlucky man does learn to work hard and diligently, if he learns to carry on sound social relationships, and if he has a good idea of how to mix business and social efforts, he'll stop being unlucky.

But since he doesn't know how to do those things, he's unlucky. And once he's been unlucky for a time, he gets more and more unlucky. He loses his confidence, which affects his dexterity and his ability. He becomes clumsy and unsure of himself. That, in turn, affects his confidence still more—all adversely. That poor unlucky man goes into a self-reinforcing tailspin of greater and greater incompetence, more and more clumsiness, and seemingly larger and larger doses of "unluck," which is really just a coined word summing up all of his unsuitability for success.

It's perfectly rational that it should begin to affect *you* as well. You associate with a clumsy person and you start to imitate his clumsiness, both physical and every other kind. Just as your simian nature encourages you to imitate successful people when you're around them, your imitative qualities make you simulate the behavior of the unlucky people around you. They're poor at their work, sloppy and unconcerned. They can't get along with their fellow workers, so you can't get along with *your* fellow workers.

In exactly the same unconscious way that you'd pick up the behavior patterns of the successful, you pick up the behavior patterns of the unsuccessful. They become second nature to you.

In turn, you start to lose confidence in your abilities. Your feelings of insecurity sap your ability to get anything done. Pretty soon, you've gone into that same self-reinforcing tailspin of failure as the unlucky people who were your role models. You have become . . . unlucky.

The sad truth: Bad luck is catching.

Don't Let It Happen to You

Do not spend one moment with losers and unlucky people. Let the unlucky stay with the unlucky. You want to be lucky because being so is one of the key ingredients of success. So you must spend your time with the lucky people of this world.

Just as a matter of course, the finalists in the life contest spend their waking moments with lucky people. You must do the same thing if you want to be lucky as well.

And if you think that you can get anywhere substantial in this world without luck, you're in for one of the bigger surprises of your life. You need luck, and you need to avoid bad luck. It's an indispensable rule of game playing.

※ ※ ※

Rule of the Game No. 4:
Life Is a Process, and the Process Never Ends

Good-bye, Johnny B. Goode

One of the most popular songs of the rich decade of the 1950s was the story of a young man from the piney backwoods of the South whose dream is to become a rock star. His father kicks him out of the house because he plays the guitar too much and too loud. So Johnny heads "for Nashville, where they say 'y'all,' and those swingin' cats are havin' a ball." There he runs into a man "with a big cigar, who says, 'C'mere kid. I'm gonna make you a star. Buy you a Cadillac, put you on Bandstand.'" And sure enough, the man with the cigar makes our boy an overnight sensation. The very next thing he knows, he's riding around in a huge Cadillac, with everything his heart desired. (It all lasts until he's drafted.)

In two minutes and five seconds of a record, this boy summarizes exactly what's at the heart of the American dream: the idea of the overnight sensation.

In America, the motivating force is not slow, steady acceleration of power, prestige, and wealth. If there's any idea that is relentlessly propagated by the American media apparatus, it is this: If you make it in America, you make it overnight. One day you're an unknown ingenue married to Norman

Maine (remember *A Star Is Born?*), and the next night you're standing in front of 50,000 screaming fans. One night you're schlepping around little clubs in Liverpool, and the next evening you're telling reporters that you're more popular than Jesus. One morning you're a refugee, penniless and ragged, and the next morning you're the head of a major conglomerate, with offices 50 floors above Columbus Circle.

This concept—that once you make it, you make it big, make it fast, make it gigantic, and all your worries are over—includes the notion that once you've started down the road to success—been found by the man with the big cigar—your momentum carries you effortlessly the rest of the way in no time at all. Once you're well on your way, you're like a ballistic missile that needs no further push once it's gone a short distance. The initial thrust is so great that the rocket is carried deep into space by itself, as it were.

That whole concept of how the world works is utterly and completely wrong. There's no sudden leap into the stratosphere of no cares and no worries. There's only advancing step by step, slowly and tortuously, up the pyramid toward your goals, which become new and more complex as you move up the ziggurat.

Life happens more in the manner of a 10,000-meter run. Every step forward is a continuing struggle. As you move farther and farther along the path, as it looks easier and easier to the people on the sidelines, it's actually harder and harder.

Allen G. is one of the most successful producers in Hollywood. When he wants to make a deal or get a studio head on the telephone, all he has to do is ask his secretary to pick up the receiver and dial. His creative judgement and business acumen are valued by filmdom from the Hollywood Freeway to Malibu. And yet . . .

When Allen G. came to Hollywood in 1975, his great goal and ambition was to get a film produced. He had a talented friend write a script and got a commitment to direct from the same friend. That was in 1976. Then, every day, almost every hour of every day, Allen ground it out, going to meeting after meeting with anyone who might possibly be able to help put a deal together. He met with people who were barely literate, people who treated him contemptuously. He persevered. "If I can just get this one picture made," he'd say, "I'll be happy. Then it will all be much, much easier. Then I'll be rolling."

After a couple of false starts, a deal was made producing Allen's picture. In itself that's a triumph, since a great many pictures are pitched each year, and only a few are made or even commenced. So Allen was in heaven. Two days later, the deal was broken when the executives of the studio left to start a new production company. Still, Allen G. persevered. He persuaded one of the department executives to make his picture as one of their first projects in their new company.

This time the deal stuck. The picture actually got made. It now exists as a successful film, which made both money and a reputation for its makers.

What is Allen's life like now? Is he floating above the cares and worries of life? "It never ends, man," is his most frequent refrain. "The aggravation, the problems, people ripping you off. It just never ends. There's a whole new set of problems that are just as infuriating as they were when I was completely outside the process, just pressing my nose against the window."

"There are no big breakthroughs," says Allen G. (who has now gotten many other production commitments). "It's all a process, and it just never ends."

Allen's situation is the distilled essence of the difference between life viewed from the inside and life viewed from the outside. From the outside, it looks as if his life is the very epitome of "the overnight sensation" at work. After all, a few years ago, he was strictly nowhere, tooling around town in a beat-up MG, without an office anywhere but in his apartment. He was just one of a million struggling producers in Hollywood. Now he has an office at a studio, where he's called by major agents every day, trying to get him to commit to deals. He has a BMW, and he looks thin and confident. He was married to an Oscar-winning star. He seems like an overnight sensation.

What takes some looking to see is that Allen G., successful Hollywood hotshot, still has to work every bit as hard as he did before he made his production deal. From the inside, Allen G. doesn't feel the slightest bit like an overnight sensation. He just feels like he's climbed up one rung of a ladder that has a great many rungs, and every rung has problems of its own.

The Big Deal Is Alive and Well in Argentina

More significant by far than the view from inside his skin is the lesson of Allen G. and those like him on the subject of "the big deal." A part of the myth of American life is that there's a certain deal, a certain accomplishment, which, after it's done, will lead to the keys to the kingdom. You see the fruits of this belief not only in America, but everywhere in the Western world. The hustler, the promoter, the schemer, and the dreamer live in a state of chronic deprivation day in and day out, just waiting for that one big deal that will make them into Donald Trump reborn or into Barbra Streisand reborn, or into Bill Gates or Oprah Winfrey. Then all their earthly cares will be at an end.

The one big deal is the exact analogy to the overnight sensation—the one big deal will put you forever beyond the reach of the pettiness, the smallness, and the harm that life can throw your way. If you can just get the job as vice president, you'll never feel any self-doubt again. If you can just put together the financing for that condominium, you'll be sailing for the rest of your life on a tranquil, glassy sea of confidence and cheer. If you can just persuade Jason, Jr., to put off leaving home to join a rock group, you'll be in hog heaven, gleefully eating out of the trough of nectar and ambrosia for the rest of time.

Often, one of the components of the one-big-deal fantasy is money. If you can somehow get together enough cash . . . that is, if, by a miracle of luck, concentration, and willpower, you can make that one big score, you'll have enough money so that you'll never again have to worry about how to pay that damned plumber or your American Express bill.

Just as often, one of the elements of the big-deal fantasy is fame or prestige. If (a *big* if) you can pull off the coup that you've been dreaming of, you'll never again have to languish in obscurity. If you can just make that one big masterstroke, you'll put yourself so far ahead of the ordinary run of humanity that you'll never have to wait at a French restaurant while the maître d' seats Angelina Jolie ahead of you even though you've been waiting for an hour. If you can just accomplish this one great event of your life, you can get such a leg up on the world that at your high school reunion you'll be greeted with bowing and scraping. The girls who ignored you back in your sophomore year will whisper enticements in your ears, if you can only pull off this one haul.

Forget about it. The entire concept of the one big deal is spurious. That one big deal may happen, and indeed, if you follow the precepts of Bunkhouse Logic, it probably *will* happen. You'll get a great deal of happiness and satisfaction from it. But it won't put you out of the need of ever having to work, suffer annoyance, get treated like dirt, feel anxiety, or get angry. There's no deal on earth so big or so successful that it will place you beyond the reach of care.

Bunkhouse Logic assures you, as surely as you live and breathe, that no one has ever pulled off such a deal. John D. Rockefeller suffered taunts and humiliations and insults even after he became the richest man in the world. J. P. Morgan was hauled before a Congressional committee and tormented even after he became the leading financier of the Western World. Franklin D. Roosevelt, the most loved President in all American history, had to go through embarrassment and pleading and cajoling even after he was elected to the nation's highest office by a hysterically adoring populace. No one escapes having to keep on working, to keep on pushing that rock up the hill, even after the greatest of great deals.

The cowboy, guiding his cattle across the plains from one feeding spot to another, knows that if he pulls off the feed and gets the cattle to the market fat and healthy, he will get paid well. And he'll probably get a bonus. He may have enough of a bonus to buy himself an F-150 and a wild weekend in Sheridan. But he knows very well that he'll simply have to make that cattle drive again next season.

He knows that the world won't come to a stop and begin acting in an entirely different way just because he pulled off his deal. He knows perfectly well that even if he discovers oil on a remote part of that land where the cattle graze, his worries aren't over. Somehow he'll have to fight to get the mineral rights, and fight with a drilling company to drill, and then fight for his proper royalty share, and then fight with the government if it tries to control the price of oil.

The cowboy, the man who lives in the bunkhouse, knows in his bones that life is a process, a continuing process in which the effort is never ending, even if it is on various different levels of satisfaction, creativity, and reward. He doesn't expect that there will ever be a deal, just *one* big deal, that will put him in the place where there are no further struggles or travails, and all life is quiet and calm.

All of life's winners know it, too. Life is an unfolding, gradual series of steps. You have to know it to win the game. Some of the steps can place you far closer to your heart's desire than others. Some of the steps may even *bring* you to your heart's desire. After all, your one big deal could be to get the man or woman you love to fall in love with you and marry you. But you should never expect that any deal, no matter how big, will put you beyond the necessity of continuing effort.

The Silver Lining

All of this talk about unending effort is a bit grim at first blush. But in fact, it's a message of good cheer. Really, it's at least *two* messages of good cheer.

First, it doesn't hurt to work. In fact, it feels good. Sentencing someone to work isn't like sentencing him to Devil's Island. Work is one of the great satisfactions of human life. No one, least of all you, should think that it's something to be avoided.

Samuel Johnson pointed out that when he was distressed or in low spirits, he found that work almost always brought him out of his slump. "Generally speaking," said the learned doctor, "labor is the surest and safest cure for the sickness of misery of the soul" (or words to that effect). You've almost certainly had similar experiences in your own life. You've had Monday mornings when you drag yourself out of the old Chevy, across the parking lot, into your office, and sit glumly down at your desk. You look around frantically for a way to avoid doing any work. Finally, you see that you must plunge into that morning's pile of correspondence. So you work at it steadily for 15 minutes by the old office clock, then you work at it for a few more minutes—and suddenly, "all the blues are gone."

In some way that has so far defied explanation by Dr. Joyce Brothers, working fortifies that spirit, banishes depression, and generally sets us up for a useful and happy day.

By the exact same token, not working makes us feel terrible. We've all seen, over and over again, people who cry out for an end to their work. They can't stand working another minute, they say. They must run off to a place where they no longer have to toil and struggle.

So, by prodigious effort and self-denial, they find the wherewithal to stop work. They take the proceeds of the house, the car, the boat, and the wife's furs, and they move to Puerto Vallarta. There they live in perfect quietude, occasionally leaving the house for a stroll along the beach, to watch the fishermen drawing in their brightly colored nets alongside the ornate wooden fishing boats. In the afternoon, they have a few tortillas and three double margaritas, and they go off to slumber land. In the evening, they watch the mariachi band, stare contemptuously at the tourists, and then go home to bed, perhaps under the starry skies of old Mexico, or perhaps under a hand-sewn cotton canopy that cost only a few dozen pesos.

But this man, this gringo living out a life of utter quietude, isn't happy. In fact, he's miserable. He hates his idleness more than he ever hated work. Next thing you know, he's back at work with his suntan, hungering for ever more assignments to feed himself and his insatiable appetite for labor. And, for the time being, he's happy.

Human beings need to work; it's a fact of the human spirit. The soul needs to feel productively engaged. That means that you must work. You need to work just as much as you need to eat or drink. So when Bunkhouse Logic assures you that you need to think of life as a process, one requiring endless labor, you shouldn't look upon it as a cruel twist of fate. It would be so if you were forbidden to work, but not if you *had* to work. Labor is for the mind and soul what jogging is for the heart and lungs: It's good for them.

The second reason why you should be glad that life is a process, never ending and infinite, is that your possibilities for satisfaction are enhanced by just exactly that much more. If you'd completed your earthly work by the time you were made head of sales for the Montgomery County region of the IBM sales matrix, you'd have very little indeed to look forward to. If you'd completed all there was to do in life by selling your first house, you'd have very little joy about what might come next.

But since life is so much more than an "on-off" switch, in which you're either "on" or "off," you can expect that all the pleasures of life will go on and on and on, forever sweeping you up in their possibilities.

Imagine life as a huge palace, like the one at Versailles, or Hugh Hefner's mansion, or the house of your Uncle Izzy—the one who was such a schlepper until he bought Belridge Oil at $80 a share, just before it went to $1,200. If life were not an unending process, you would expect that after a great deal of effort and concentration and self-sacrifice, you would make it into one of the beautiful, ornate rooms of the palace.

What a sight! The room would be a pale yellow, with gold-leaf inlay along the floor molding. The ceiling would have been painted 400 years ago by an artist with such exquisite sensibilities that now they cannot find anyone even to repair some of the faded tracery. Along the gracefully curved corners of the room would be elaborate solid-gold bas-reliefs of the sacking of Troy. On each wall would be an original Rembrandt, flanked by an original Botticelli. In the center of the room you'd see Yo-Yo Ma playing one of Beethoven's more delicate piano concerti on his cello.

That is what the room of success, the room of breakthrough, looks like. It's beautiful.

But frankly, you get sick of it after a few days. Imagine if the Fates sentenced you to spend all your time in such a room. Even a room as beautiful as that would get depressing indeed.

Your prayers are answered. The room with the cherubim on the ceiling is not your final destination (at least not while you're alive). Life is a process, and you have the opportunity to go through all the rooms of the palace. You can see and touch all kinds of different rooms and places. And the effort involved in experiencing all that variety will be more than worthwhile.

Because life is a process, it's always unfolding and new. The successful of this world relish that opportunity to constantly see that there is novelty and diversion in a world that would otherwise seem weary, stale, flat, and unprofitable.

The cowboy, heading up toward the rodeo, knows that each bull he rides is a different animal, with different sensibilities. Each time he's thrown—either before or after the whistle—he'll feel something he didn't feel before. The cowboy looks forward to that variety in his life. He wouldn't want just to win one big bull-riding contest and then sit on the sidelines for the rest of his life. He wants to see and do new things—and so should you.

Life is a seamless web of movement, forward and backward. It requires endless movement and effort. There's no big deal that will keep you from ever having to toil again. The concept of the paradisal easy street is a myth.

But this prospect is cheering rather than frightening. Work and effort are rewards in themselves. They shouldn't be avoided any more than you'd avoid healthy, wholesome exercise.

Moreover, the fact that life is a process means that there are opportunities for endless variety and novelty in what would otherwise be a boring consumption of our allotted time.

Life is a process and it never ends. Expect it and be glad about it. Bear it in mind as you play the game. It will bring you out ahead.

※ ※ ※

Rule of the Game No. 5:
Nothing Happens by Itself

Three Parables about Doing It Yourself

Parable No. 1: J.G. is one of the most successful financial writers in America. He's had three best-selling books published, and he's the founder of several widely read financial newsletters. He was once the financial columnist for a highly respected men's magazine.

About five years ago, J.G. wanted to invest some of his money in a way that would make it grow rapidly so that he might soon retire. He'd spent a great many years living in Los Angeles and foresaw its spectacular real-estate boom. "I could see that the area around UCLA, Westwood, was going to become like a second downtown for L.A.," he says, "and it would become phenomenally valuable."

J.G. and four friends went into a venture to buy a large and (they thought) undervalued office building in Westwood, right on Wilshire Boulevard. They negotiated a fine price, secured a loan at a ridiculously low interest rate, and soon owned the building. But because all five of the partners had other work that took up their time, they needed to hire a manager of the building to supervise its tenants and run it economically. J.G. and his friends found a man who'd managed buildings for a large bank for many years. The man had a fine reputation, but was sick of working for large organizations. So he was lured away by a high salary and promise of participation in the profits of the building when it was sold.

That was five years ago. In that time, real estate in the Westwood area has generally increased in value by a large factor. J.G. and his friends decided to sell out. They went to a real-estate broker and asked him to appraise their building. The broker investigated and came back with some surprising news. "The building had actually gone down in value," J.G. says. "We couldn't believe it. How could it have happened? It turned out that the manager, this priceless jewel, had rented almost all of the building for 20 years to a bank at 1997 prices. So whoever owns the building in 2017 is still going to get 1997 rents. There was no way anybody could make money on that building. The manager just had no idea that we would ever sell it. After all, the bank he'd worked for never sold its buildings."

J.G. and his friends sold at a loss, while every building around them had become invaluable.

Parable No. 2: After he became first consul and then emperor of France, Napoléon Bonaparte conquered all of western Europe. From Spain to the Elbe River in Germany, Europe was under the control of the great Corsican genius. Napoleon had many plans for the world, including major architectural and legal edifices in France. Accordingly, he placed his friends and relatives in charge of his conquests. He made a brother the king of Rome, another brother the king of Spain, and marshals from his campaigns became princes in other countries under his control. He retired to contemplate the future.

Within 12 months, Europe was ablaze. Revolts broke out in Holland, Spain, Italy, and everywhere that Napoleon had won his great victories, so he had to stop his governance and go back to the field of battle. He defeated all of the rebellions and added still more territory to the empire, but the pattern remained: Napoleon left his relatives and friends in change of his territories, and revolts erupted.

This pattern, of Napoleon winning wars and his relatives and friends losing them, continued for all of his life, until he ventured to entrust his empire to subordinates while he conquered Russia. The little genius, considered by many to be the most able man in recent history, ended his days on a barren rock in the ocean.

Parable No. 3: Jacqueline Susann was an obscure housewife, the spouse of a successful agent. She wrote a funny book about her pet poodle, called *Every Night, Josephine!* Susann sold it to a publisher, who promised he would do great things with it. To the author's disbelief, however, the publisher did absolutely nothing with the book. The publisher could barely get the book into bookstores, let alone get it displayed or promoted. Perhaps the publisher simply had other things on his mind. In any event, the publisher responded to Susann's entreaties by promising to do more. She visited the bookstores once again, but there were still no books on the shelves.

This time, Susann armed herself with ambition. She systematically went from bookstore to bookstore to tell the managers about her book. If the managers were at all receptive, she persuaded them to display her book prominently and push it as a gift. For over a year, she traveled around the country peddling her books from one bookstore to the next, paying for her own travel, and cajoling people who were less than fascinated to get her book into the display windows.

Eventually, *Every Night, Josephine!* became a bestseller. After that, Jacqueline Susann could do no wrong, and she became one of the most successful authors in recent American history. She was incapable of writing a book that didn't become a bestseller. She did it the same way each time. Either by herself or by proxy, she went into every bookstore and simply insisted that her books be displayed, advertised, and pushed. She never relied on anyone except herself to get her books before the reading public. She became rich, and was very proud of herself. When she passed away, her name had become synonymous with literary commercial success on a stupendous scale.

Here's my point: In this life, it's almost certain that you harbor the deep-seated hope that somebody else will do it for you. No matter what "it" is, you hope that you'll be spared the ugly necessity of doing it for yourself. You all pray that the goodies of life will somehow come your way because of someone else's exertions. At the least, you likely expect that a bare minimum of work will be done on your behalf by someone else, sometime in your life.

It is no more than human to hope against hope that before you die, someone will move the chess piece that is yourself a few places along the board without your having to break your back with labor to get it done.

But Jackie Susann was smarter than Napoleon. She knew what he did not: Nothing happens by itself. Everything you want to get done, you must do by and for yourself. Jackie Susann was no great shakes as a novelist, nor was she a genius in understanding the craftsmanship of the English language. But she understood the way the world worked better than the greatest military and political genius in modern history.

You hope that you won't have to do everything yourself, but Jackie Susann was wise enough to know that the hope was in vain. J.G. understood money and movement of great economic currents, but he knew too little about the human spirit. Jackie Susann knew the human heart to perfection.

No one would tell you that Napoleon's exploits should be ignored. And your author would certainly not want to slight J.G. But there should be a statue to Jacqueline Susann right at the corner of Fifth Avenue and 59th Street. The inscription on the plaque should read: "She knew how to do it herself."

※ ※ ※

The world is rich in possibilities. It overflows with the good things that humankind has created for itself. They're out there for the taking. But before you learn how to take them, you must first learn that no one will do it for you.

Bunkhouse Logic tells you that you can accomplish masterworks of creativity and enterprise that you never dreamed of. You can go from the file room to the executive suite in record time. You can go from the laundry room of your apartment house to the Côte d'Azur. You can get ahead of all those twerps from your class back at Podunk State U. But you can only do those things if you understand that you have to do them for yourself.

Once again, imagine the cowboy leading his herds along the dusty plains of western Oklahoma, far from any comforts or conveniences. He has his portable radio and canned food and his old pickup truck, but that's about all. The herd must be brought to market, or years of effort will go down the drain. The cowboy knows, right down to his Justin boots, that if he doesn't shoulder the responsibility of getting those steers to market, those steers will not *get* to market.

The cowboy knows, as we all should, that his job is to herd cattle. He cannot logically expect anyone else to do it for him. If he doesn't do it himself, then good-bye, cattle; good-bye, job; and most important of all, good-bye, self-respect.

The cowboy doesn't simply abandon his cattle 20 miles from the market and wait to see if they arrive by themselves. He herds them every inch of the way.

Similarly, your ideas, your creativity, and your energy are your charges. You cannot just abandon them to the free play of the cruel world. You must guide them and take care of them by doing for yourself. That is how you win the game.

Think enough of yourself to *do* for yourself. That is how you'll thrive in the world, and that's the only way.

The Way It Goes

The world is a callous and disorganized place. It's also a highly self-centered place. Let's not kid ourselves. It doesn't care that much whether you get ahead or not. The world will keep going in its accustomed chaotic style perfectly well without your ascent to fame or stardom or wealth or a happy home or any of the goals you have in mind. Every 24 hours, the earth revolves upon its axis. It will continue to do so even if you're hoping desperately that it will stop and take note of you.

Just as the earth's movements on its axis and in its orbit go on without much regard for us as individuals, so too do the other people in this world go on without much regard for us as individuals. But the world doesn't have to work that way. You can make the world take some notice of your existence and even of your wants.

If you want to have that lovely home in Darien, Connecticut, with the white-picket fence and the children who grow up as fine, caring human beings, you can do it. It can definitely happen. But you must *make* it happen. It won't happen by itself. The world will allow you to take the things you want and need from it. But the world won't give them to you of its own accord.

Nothing happens by itself. Everything can happen if you make it happen.

※ ※ ※

Rule of the Game No. 6:
The Best Is the Enemy of the Good

Perfectionism—The Great Crippler of Young Adults

Al Burton was the director of creative affairs for one of the largest TV producers in Hollywood. He witnessed the elevation of television from a small experiment into the most powerful media apparatus in all history. From his offices on Sunset Boulevard, he supervised production for prime-time television situation comedies.

Each and every day, Burton saw young men and women parading into his office with stars in their eyes. They wanted to be great men and women of the flickering screen. They had ideas of how they would make television into a completely new and different force.

"These people came in here with tons of energy, just waiting and dying to become someone important and get their ideas across on TV—and make that kind of money that you make for writing successfully for TV," Burton remarked. "Some of them made it," he added while playing with a weather radio on his small Louis XV–reproduction desk, "and most of them went back to Kankakee."

But could he predict which of them would make it in advance of their actually doing so? "To a certain extent," he said. "This is how I could tell. If a guy came in here with his heart pouring out a desire to write a script for 'a show,' I had it in my power to tell him to write an outline of a story. If we liked the story, he'd get money for the story outline, and then he'd get money for the story—the script—when he wrote it.

"I made that offer about 20 times each month," Burton said. "And most people took that possibility and went home and just got completely frozen. They thought that they had to turn out the greatest script in the history of television. They sat at their typewriters and they tried to write the one dynamite first line of stage direction that was going to make them immortal. And it didn't come out that way. So they tried about a hundred different ways of writing that first line or that first act, and all the time they were trying to be the Molière of situation comedy, trying to write something that would be absolutely perfect.

"They're the ones who went back to Kankakee," he continued, "because they were the ones who were never going to turn in anything at all. They got so completely wound up with trying to do something perfect that they never did anything at all. I would see them maybe a year later and they'd tell me they were still working on that sitcom script, and God help them, it was the truth."

Burton looked at a Delacroix reproduction painting of a Parisian street scene and smiled a contagious grin. "The ones who were going to make it were the ones who took home a few copies of scripts that had already aired and tried to do one at just about the level that you see on TV every night. They didn't try to do junk, and they didn't try to do Shakespeare. They just wanted to do a workmanlike, solid, good job. And that's what they did. And those guys might come back here 20 times trying to do the same show, but eventually they'd get one on the air that would fly. Then they'd be off to the races."

Al added, "The ones who made it are the ones who weren't killed by thinking that they had to be the one perfect Hollywood TV writer. The ones who made it just wanted to be good enough to get one on the tube."

Well said, Mr. Burton, my dear friend. Few things can be more wasteful of time and spirit than the necessity of having to live up to a completely irrelevant and useless standard of perfection. The compulsion to do something perfect is the exact equivalent of the compulsion never to get anything done at all. Both of them lead to a hopeless lack of production. If nothing is produced, nothing is accomplished, and no steps are taken to getting you the objects of your heart's desire.

The problem applies in every other field in addition to television scriptwriting. Imagine that you're just starting out in the syndication department of a bank. Your job is to find the lowest rate for placing tombstone newspaper advertisements. But you secretly want to form syndicates. At night you lie on your Serta Perfect Sleeper imagining how much you'd enjoy dreaming up the smartest syndicates in investment history.

You think so hard, in fact, that you get panicky. Ideas occur to you, but you have to admit that they aren't perfect. You want to go to your boss with an idea, but you want it to be one that will be worshiped at Harvard Business School for generations. The idea, the perfect idea, just doesn't come to you. Lots of perfectly good syndication ideas occur to you, but they're not quite perfect. So time goes by, and you do nothing.

You poor fool. No one forms perfect syndicates. Absolutely no one. No one expects your suggestions to be perfect. All they have to be is good enough. Go out there and deluge you boss with your hundreds of good ideas. You'll be far better off than if you stayed in your cubbyhole forever trying to come up with that one perfect syndication concept.

Do not allow your search for the best to keep you from producing the good. The good will be good enough to get you where you want to go.

The cowboy, guiding his herds of cattle to market, doesn't attempt to do his job perfectly. He doesn't expect to have his longhorns and his Herefords separated and marching down the prairie in perfect order like North Korean soldiers. Instead, he just wants to get those cattle to market. If he can do it with a minimum of difficulty, he will have done well. He'll be promoted and paid for it. He doesn't have to go into his tent and sulk all night because he lost one calf to a rattlesnake. He never expected to do his work perfectly. He just had to get it done by activity and inner mobility. If he broods about being less than perfect, he accomplishes nothing, which is just what he doesn't want to do. Down in his weary bones, the cowboy knows that he'll just waste a precious lifetime dwelling on perfection. If he can do his job in a good manner, that will be plenty.

Imitate that old trail hand. Just forget about doing the best work that was ever done. That struggle will be fruitless and more: It will keep you from doing any good at all. Be active. Be inwardly mobile. Get it done. Don't think about perfection.

The best is the enemy of the good. Don't seek to do the impossible. Do the good, the possible, and that will suffice for anything at all, including moving along life's one-way street to the object of your desires—whatever that may be.

The best is the enemy of the good. All the winning players know it as a rule of the game.

※ ※ ※

Rule of the Game No. 7:
Personal Relationships Are Golden

It's Not What You Know . . .

School teaches many things. If you're lucky, you learned to read and write in that old brick schoolhouse. Perhaps you learned a bit of arithmetic and maybe even some algebra. You learned the fate of the six wives of Henry VIII, and you learned how Impressionism turned into Pointillism. You learned how to study for exams, and if you were especially disciplined, you learned how to write a neat and clear essay in the English language.

Each year you advanced through school, merrily taking your examinations and your tests. If you passed those rather elementary puzzles, you were automatically advanced into the next grade. This process continued whether or not you were the slightest bit aware of your surroundings or the people who were in your class. A boy or girl of middling intelligence could readily make it all the way to the top of the Ph.D. program in public policy at Harvard University with only the vaguest idea of how to get along with that fellow who sat next to him in Problems of Eastern Europe all year. A woman with the ability to study assiduously could make it comfortably all the way into high honors at UC Berkeley in English literature without any notion of how to be a friend to the people who lived near her in the dormitory.

But make no mistake: In life after school, personal relationships are crucial. And the further complication is that most people are utterly unprepared for this huge fact of life: If you're a failure in your personal relationships, you're likely to be a failure in everything.

Personal relationships are the fertile soil from which all advancement, all success, and all achievement in real life grows. Without the ability to become friends with people, to get along easily with the folks around you, to inspire confidence in men and women above and below you, to be trusted—let's face it, to be a good guy or girl—you simply can't get anywhere.

Think of Henry Kissinger. This man was undoubtably the greatest foreign-affairs thinker of our time. He was able to analyze the world situation steps ahead of any secretary of state you might want to mention. But although Kissinger was the greatest of thinkers, he wasn't the *only* genius in foreign affairs at Harvard. And there were others at Princeton and MIT and Columbia and Yale and Stanford and the American Enterprise Institute. Why, then, did Kissinger advance so dramatically to the forefront of his field?

I'll tell you why. Because he became friends with certain persons who could do him a lot of good. Kissinger knew not only why the Congress of Vienna was a great success, but also why and how to get along perfectly with Nelson A. Rockefeller, who plucked him from Harvard to help write his Rockefeller Panel Reports on defense and foreign policy. Other scholars might have been chosen to work on these reports—as they were—but Kissinger made the most of the opportunity. He knew very well indeed that he'd been handed the golden opportunity of his life. There was simply no way that a friendship with Nelson Rockefeller would *not* turn into a fantastic ticket to advance into the world where real decisions are made about life-and-death matters.

So Kissinger did whatever was necessary to cement his friendship with Rockefeller. Kissinger was so smart that he knew that his encyclopedic knowledge of foreign affairs and his thorough grasp of politics weren't enough. Personal relationships were the keys that unlocked the important doors.

Later in Kissinger's life, he was picked out of the Rockefeller entourage to work for the one who actually made it to the White House. Many of Rockefeller's spear-carriers sought refuge in their academic meanderings, barely acknowledging the loss by their candidate. Not so Henry the K. When he was asked to meet Richard Nixon, once the hate object of the Rockefeller clique, Kissinger poured on the charm.

Kissinger was smart enough to know that no amount of posturing as the world's smartest man would do any good. He had to make Nixon believe that he, Kissinger, really liked him. And, in fact, Kissinger probably *did* like him. Kissinger was so much of a genius in the ways of the world that he knew in his gut that he was going nowhere with the new administration unless he and Nixon became buddies.

The result was that Kissinger made Nixon his teammate. The two of them became the most formidable President/foreign-affairs advisor team in American history. And Kissinger, who might have been just another smart refugee grinding out lectures at Harvard, became a worldwide celebrity and a man who guided the fortunes of the democratic world.

Once again, there were people who knew almost as much as he did. There were those who had more astounding academic records. But Henry Kissinger had the smarts to know that personal relationships were the key to everything. That's why he was a superstar and others were academic hacks.

If Kissinger knew this kind of thing, it pretty much had to be correct. Everyone can think of a hundred—no, a thousand—examples of just how much personal relationships mean in any field of endeavor. You've seen what Kissinger saw: that your ties on a human-to-human basis in this world are what get you ahead. But in the past, you haven't necessarily drawn the correct conclusions: that you must redouble your efforts to forge good personal relationships with those around you.

There's no one who's so smart, so virtuous, so good-looking, and so rich that he can advance all the way across the board on the basis of those looks, money, brains, and so forth alone. It's also a life-and-death matter to make friends with people. Only out of those friendships will the fruits of true success blossom forth.

It happens every day. There you are in the traffic section of BBDO. You want to get out of there and get into more creative work at the agency. Or you want to get out of there and get to be an account executive. You know full well that you're the smartest person you know, especially in the traffic department. How, then, do you get out of that pit and into something more appealing? Partly, you decide what you want. Partly, you ask for what you want. Partly, you step up to the table, with the sure and certain knowledge that you can't win if you're not at the table.

But once you're at the table, you form good personal relationships with the people around you—those who can and will help you if only you give them the slightest incentive to be your friend—and if you make them help you (bearing in mind that nothing happens by itself). This is the best of all possible worlds, as Dr. Pangloss said, but it's still highly imperfect. If the world were run perfectly, perhaps you would be promoted, advanced, and rewarded on the basis of sheer ability. But the world doesn't work that way—or even close to that way.

When your superiors look for someone to promote, they look for someone they know and like. When the hiring partner at the law firm looks for a new associate, he most certainly looks at the candidate's academic record. But he also consults his feelings to see how he feels about the applicant. You can feel confident indeed that the young lawyer who made friends with old Mr. Crouchbotham, the hiring partner, will soon find himself with a desk at Cravath, Swaine & Moore. The fellow who was totally brilliant but offered no form of human warmth will find himself stuck in the library stacks.

You want to get ahead. You want to get those achievements under your belt so that you can feel confident and happy about yourself. There's nothing wrong with that. It's the essence of the human condition. But Bunkhouse Logic admonishes you that you must put yourself in the other fellow's shoes. Think how much you'd like to promote someone you like. Think how much you would *not* like to promote a cold fish. Then go out and make yourself likable. That's just how the winning players play the game.

The cowboy, waiting around the ranch for the next cattle drive, knows that certain routes are more painful and less rewarding than others. He knows very well that the trail boss has in his power the assignment of routes. The cowboy doesn't expect that he'll get the safest, best route just because he's a good trail hand. He also knows, just as a matter of human nature, that if the trail boss likes him, he'll get far better assignments than if the trail boss does *not* like him. Once again, that is no more or less than human nature. The cowboy doesn't question it for a moment.

You shouldn't question it either. Those powerful people who can confer favors that will change and enrich your life like to confer them on people they like. An elementary Rule of the Game! Make sure you are one of them.

No Brownnosers Need Apply

Bunkhouse Logic emphatically tells you that there's no need to be sycophantic in forming your personal relationships. Most people are so eager to have friends of any kind that they hardly require having ones who will kiss their asses. From your own experience, you can tell that life is often so lonely that any friends at all are a godsend. To have friends who are endlessly kissing up to you is more of a bother than a pleasure.

The cowboy out on the trail knows that if his trail boss requires constant apple-polishing and flattery, the cowboy had better find a new trail boss. So it is in real life in the big city or suburbs. When you meet the rare person who needs major brownnosing, you might just as well stay the hell away.

Any person, man or woman, whom you want to be your friend is worth knowing if he or she will accept sincere, straightforward friendship. Extortion of servility is a sign of such bad character that you want nothing to do with such a person.

In addition, constant ass-kissing is so demeaning to the ass-kisser and the ass-kissed that it cheapens life. If you have to do it in your field, find another field. Life is simply too short to be a courtier in a democracy.

"Ron David," a powerful headhunter at a leading recruitment firm, likes to say that while employers want to hire the best people they can, " . . . they really like the best man or woman they know."

The difference is crucial to understanding why personal relationships are so important. In a world in which criteria are often subjective and uncertain, it is helpful indeed to know the powers in your chosen field. Human beings want to like people. Humans as a group want to help those they like and the people who like them, and you want to help your friends. That means that it's vital to be a friend to the people who can help you.

Bunkhouse Logic tells you that the great mass of opportunities for work and personal creative satisfaction arise from personal relationships. This is exactly the opposite of the routine you learned in school, but it's obviously true, nevertheless. In school, personal relationships mean nothing in advancement. In life after school, they mean everything. The cowboy knows this. So should you.

Life is largely a process of seduction. You must seduce favors and chances for achievement out of people. It's not strange that the same tools required for love should be required for success in any field. Everyone who can confer a favor, after all, wants to be loved.

Finally, even if you cannot know everyone in your field intimately, you must let your face and name be known so that the movers and shakers of the world have an incentive to choose you when they look for the best person "they know."

Personal relationships are golden. They're the winning chips in the game of getting what you want from life.

※ ※ ※

Rule of the Game No. 8:
Persistence

The One Indispensable Ingredient

If all the great men and women of all time were put into a giant calculator that reduced all of their personality traits to a numerical equivalent, you'd still have a large and complex number. If you then wanted to find the common denominator of personalities of all the great winners, the one great Rule of the Game embedded in their characters, you'd find it in this single characteristic: persistence.

Successful men and women come in all shapes, sizes, and colors. They reach their goals at differing stages of life and at varying levels of health, wealth, and wisdom. Some are attractive and some are not. But they're all persistent people.

If there were some way that persistence could be determined in advance so that those who had it would give off a particular brilliance, this brilliance would be a perfect predictor of who was likely to reach his or her heart's desire.

The simple fact of life is that there are so many twists and turns; and so much delay, quibbling, deception, trickery, chagrin, and deceit, that nothing ever goes as you hope and plan.

There's no one at all—movie star, billionaire, rock musician, artist, composer, advertising magnate—who escapes frustration and disappointment. It just isn't a part of the human condition. The common lot of the human animal is to struggle, work, sacrifice, and be cruelly tricked by fate. This is the nature of the game.

Where the truth comes in is how differing human beings respond to these things. Those who will triumph meet the trials of life, endure them, and persist. The people who see the caveats of life and make caviar will succeed in both the long and the short runs. The men and women who stay in the race even when the track has vicious twists and turns are the ones who will reach the finish line of their dreams. They know that the Rules of the Game demand persistence as an indispensable ingredient.

There is, quite simply, no substitute for perseverance in meeting the trials of the day—except failure. If you hope to succeed, you're not in a position to persist or to fail to persist. Your only choice is persistence or oblivion. The people who attain their goals are the ones who have persisted in fighting for what they want. The ones who hang from straps in the subway with blank looks on their faces are the ones who didn't persist and gave in to defeat.

Everyone can expect to be defeated repeatedly on a temporary basis. It's inevitable that some defeat will enter even the most victorious life. The human spirit is never finished when it's defeated, though. It's finished when it quits. That, I learned from Richard Nixon.

Those who abandon persistence are those who will lead wasted lives. Those who cling to their dreams until they realize their dreams are those who will inevitably come out of the games with some gold medals. The price will be high, as it always is, but the day when you clamber over the last craggy rock and look down into the sunlit valley of accomplishment will certainly dawn upon you eventually.

A relentless persistence is like a steel beam running through the structure of your life. As long as it's in place, even the most severe buffetings will leave the structure basically intact. But once that invincible support is gone, the house will collapse with the next strong wind. And the winds will surely come as you make your way to your heart's desire. But your persistence will get you through them. If you have no persistence, you can say good-bye to all your hopes, dreams, and wishes—all the accomplishments that will make you feel truly proud of yourself.

Without the determination to go forward, you simply stop going forward. You lose all sense of momentum. You can easily be blown right off course by a sneer from a producer, a turndown from the head of accounts receivable, or any number of small (or large) vicissitudes. Once you're blown off course, you have no point of reference. Your entire life becomes a series of parries and ripostes to day-by-day incidents. You lose sight of your major goals and wishes in your overwhelming need to simply meet each day's trials.

Without persistence, you have no psychic wellspring of strength to combat what life will throw at you. You huddle endlessly in the foxhole of failure, cowering at each new artillery report.

Don't let it happen. If you have persistence, you can put yourself back on course within a decade, if a decade is how long it takes you to get where you want to go. With that key inner support, you can place yourself in a position to rebuild your house when it's been scorched by the fires of defeat.

With persistence, you can always see your goal looming ahead, no matter how far away. Without persistence, there's no hope of triumph. As long as you have your persistence, anything is possible. Without persistence, no lasting accomplishment is possible.

If the Rules of the Game are what physical conditioning is to an athlete, then *persistence* as a Rule of the Game is your heart. Without its steady beating nothing is possible.

❀ ❀ ❀

Rule of the Game No. 9:
Make Time Your Ally

Nor Call Back Time in Its Winged Flight . . .

One of the most tragically unfair contests of human life is the struggle between the human spirit and time. Men and women throw their hearts and souls into the effort to get somewhere. They rush headlong, pell-mell into the fracas to wrest whatever success they can from life in the shortest possible space of time. They hurl themselves against the clock to attempt to coax another few morsels of achievement out of the moment before that moment has passed.

As a human being, you run a deadly race against time. You know that your allotted span of years will be brief, always shorter than you would have wanted, and you seek to blast out of those years all of the goodies of life you can. In this primal struggle, you use up your health, your peace of mind, and your serenity. In order to defeat the clock, you throw away the magnificence of life with both hands.

Sometimes you may set deadlines: "I will be a successful writer in Hollywood within X years." "I will have that house in Newport Beach within Y years." "I will be the head of the buying department at Bergdorf's within Z years." You grasp at every straw and every expedient to make those deadlines. If it takes becoming a chain-smoker, you'll do it. If it takes gastric colitis to do it, so be it. If it takes endless depressed weekends, you'll endure that, too.

You *will* call back time in its winged flight. You *will* make time do your bidding. You *will* impose your will on time.

It never happens. Time is the master of us all.

Bunkhouse Logic tells you that you should want to achieve. Bunkhouse Logic tells you that you should want to accomplish all that you can. Bunkhouse Logic is the approximate science of getting what you want by betting on yourself and winning.

But Bunkhouse Logic will never tell you to wage war against time. In the struggle against time, there's only one possible winner. No one can defeat time. No one can make time his slave. You cannot call back time in its winged flight. No one can overmaster time or make time his handmaiden. Time is the supreme ruler of everyone's life. Bunkhouse Logic would never tell anyone to even attempt to conquer time.

Far from it. Bunkhouse Logic tells you that the only way to wage your life successfully is to make time your ally. By doing so, the whole problem of accomplishing and achieving takes on a new ease and grace. With time on your side, you can acquire a new serenity about how life will flow, and how the rewards will flow from that new serene life.

What does it mean to make time your ally? Many things.

It means that you must never rush the natural rhythm of life. You should not live in slow motion, but neither should you attempt to impose your own speed on an immense planet. There's a pace to the affairs of human beings. Let that be your pace as well. Don't break yourself on the rack of frustration by trying to do more in less time than anyone has ever done. Instead of battling time, let time carry you.

The need to make time your ally goes hand in hand with every other rule. The indispensable partner of every Bunkhouse Logician is a sense that there will be enough time to get the job done. Racing against that time is simply futile. Making time work for you is neither more nor less than a pleasurable necessity.

Bob B., a hugely successful Hollywood producer, told of how making time his ally put the decisive touch on his own quest for those golden personal relationships.

"When I came to Hollywood," he said, "a wise man told me that I should make a list of the hundred people I wanted to meet. As soon as I made the list, I realized that I could meet most of them within a few months. That would be about 80 percent of them. Then I could reach the next

10 percent in about a year, just letting things flow at a leisurely schedule, running into people at parties and screenings.

"I went to the wise man. I told him that I figured it would take two years to meet all of the people I wanted to meet. 'I'm in a hurry,' I told him. 'I want to move on this right away.' The wise man looked at me, smiled, and said, 'Pal, the way to make sure that you never happen at all in this town is to rush it. If you play it slow and easy, eventually everything will come your way. If you try to jam that square peg into that round hole, nothing will come your way.'"

Bob laughed as he told this story. "As it happened, it took about three years to meet the people. Some of them crossed my path when I was going somewhere or they were going somewhere, and it just wasn't the right time to meet. But most of them just fell right into place. I didn't force myself on them, and they didn't resent me for it. It worked out beautifully, just the way he said it would."

On the wall of Bob's office there's a sign that tells the whole story: *Hay tiempo,* it says. *There is time.*

Life is short. The temptation is to rush everything to get it done within the space of a lifetime. That's exactly the way to always come out behind. If you flow along the river of time, working at its own pace, you find that time stretches out indefinitely. So do opportunities. If you don't make time your ally, and instead fight against it, you only fill your days with anguish and disappointment. Add a measure of grace by making time your ally, and you'll be amazed by how much more life will have to offer—and how beautifully it will be served up to you.

Time is as much a primal element of life as water or air. You breathe air in and out. You need water in your system to live. But more than either of these things, you need time.

You can live briefly without air or water, but without time, there's nothing. Time is overwhelming, omnipotent, and ubiquitous in its power. It's there to be used and enjoyed. But it may never be conquered or defeated. Bunkhouse Logic advises you to forego the effort.

Live with time on your side. Life will change richly for the better. In addition, you'll move just as far along life's one-way street as you want, without the pain of warring against time. All things will come in time, but from the vain battle *against* time, nothing lasting will come forth.

Let It Bleed

The saving grace of this whole Bunkhouse Logic philosophy of activism and achievement that asks so much of your time is this: You do not have to do it all at once. *Hay tiempo.* You can rest and recoup your strength for the battles to come.

Inevitably, although tragically, you'll find that people in this world will hurt you. There are plenty of men and women with knives and forks and empty plates. When you come along, they'll cut you. More than that, life is difficult. If you're to go out into the arena and wage combat for success, life will unavoidably hand you a few good kicks right in the teeth. You'll find blood flowing from your guts more often than you care to imagine.

William Safire, the famous newspaper columnist, once explained to me that life was simply overflowing with opportunities to get your brains beaten in by the forces of indifference and hostility. "You're constantly diving into a bucket of sand from a hundred feet up," he said. "You get a bloody head pretty often."

So true, so true. When you come up bloody, as you eventually will, Bunkhouse Logic doesn't tell you to run right out and get beaten again. Instead, the logic of the bunkhouse tells you to follow the words of an old Scottish border ballad:.

> "I am wounded," cried Andrew to his merry men,
> "But I am not slain.
> I will lay me down and bleed awhile,
> Then rise to fight with you again."

There's frightening wisdom in Sir Andrew. When you're wounded, let it bleed for a while. Even the hardiest cowboy cannot just spring to his feet after he gets knocked down by a crazed bronco. Take a look at a real Western rodeo. Most of the time the cowboys riding broncos or bulls *do* get thrown. If the fall is particularly nasty, the cowboy doesn't just leap to his feet. He lies there on the ground for a minute or two to get back his wind. Then he goes right back to the pen and starts his turn for another bull.

Take a leaf from ol' Tex's book. When you go to your boss at Ogilvy & Mather and tell her that you're sick to death of doing rate cards for out-of-town clients, and then tell her that you could write better copy asleep than most copywriters can while they're awake, don't expect your boss to shower you with rose petals. More likely, she'll say, "Get back to your desk if you want to have a job when you come in tomorrow."

That hurts. Figuratively, it will bleed. You stagger back to your desk, with your ambitions writhing under the ton of concrete that your boss has just dumped on them. Don't expect to feel like going in there and asking one more time.

Let it bleed. Take some time to let your wounds heal before you go back into the arena.

And what if you're trying to teach your husband that he must stay home and help Johnny with his homework, instead of going out to watch Monday Night Football with the boys? He looks at you menacingly and says, "I didn't sign up to be a teacher, toots." Then he stalks out. Of course you're furious over his behavior. He's dumped the issue of Junior's education right on your already-burdened shoulders. You're crushed by his callousness toward you. You're bleeding.

Bunkhouse Logic tells you that you shouldn't just zip right back up onto the stage and continue fighting. Instead, you should go to your favorite chair, sit down, and let the wounds heal. Take time to let the bleeding stop of its own accord. When it does, you can take up the cudgels again.

Or, say that you're working as a summer associate at a major Wall Street law firm. You get your first assignment, which is to write a memo on a treacherous landlord-tenant tax problem, in which state and federal laws differ on how much tax can be allocated to each party. With great enthusiasm, you march to the law library. For days you research the problem through Corpus Juris, Am Jur, the USCA, the New York State Code, innumerable law reporters, and on and on. After two weeks, you have a tightly woven mesh of facts in order to explain the law to the partner.

He reads your memo and tosses it back into your lap. "This," he says, "is the worst piece of crap I've ever seen. I can't believe that a top law student did that."

You cannot quit right that minute because you've already spent your next few paychecks (a mistake in itself). You slink down to your office. What do you do? Do you go to the senior partner and complain to him about the unbelievable rudeness of the partner in question? Do you run back into the law library to get new research material? Do you run out to Herman's World of Sporting Goods to buy a pistol?

No. You go back to your office and let it bleed. You recoup your strength for the next round of battle. You sulk about life's unfairness for an hour or two, and then you go forth to conquer once again.

When you make time your ally, you realize that there's time to recover from your wounds before you go forth to fight and struggle again. There's always time to bind up your wounds and get ready for the next contest. If you try to go right back into the ring after you've just been bloodied, you won't be up to the contest. You'll just get bloodied again. But if you rest for a moment or two—or an hour, or a day, or a week—you'll soon find that you're back in fighting shape again.

You have time to recover. You don't have time to go out and fight before you do so.

It might seem that Bunkhouse Logic requires you to act harshly toward yourself. After all, the logic of the cowboy permits no excuses for failing to get the things that you've always wanted. Bunkhouse Logic tells you not to make excuses for failing, but instead to go out and succeed. Bunkhouse Logic assures you that you have to do it all yourself.

The cowboy, methodically driving his flocks along the range, doesn't try to flagellate himself into a state of nirvana. He simply does what he has to do. So it should be with Bunkhouse Logic. You can order yourself to get the things that you want from life. But one of the things you want is not to be a nervous wreck or a cardiac case in your 30s. The logic of the cattle drive and the bunkhouse tells you to get it done, but it certainly doesn't tell you to kill yourself doing it.

Hay tiempo. There is time.

Yes, sometimes you have to play while you're hurt, but only when it's absolutely unavoidable. Do not tape up your ribs and fill yourself with codeine and steroids, then rush into the Oakland Raiders' front line. There's no need. There's time to wait until you've recovered enough so that you can struggle without murdering yourself.

Life can have infinitely more opportunity when you don't fight against time. Don't try to fight this invincible element. Instead, make time your ally.

※ ※ ※

Rule of the Game No. 10:
Nice Guys Finish First

The Face in the Mirror

In the spring of 1940, the Nazi war machine crashed across the German-French border into France. Although France had the largest army in western Europe, outnumbering the Germans two-to-one in many places, the Germans rapidly broke through. Within six weeks, the government of the Third Republic sued for peace. While the French leaders generally became so demoralized that they simply agreed to whatever price the Nazis asked, one Frenchman refused to capitulate.

General Charles de Gaulle, a brigadier general in the tank corps, took as many of his men as possible and joined the British Expeditionary Force, which was fleeing to the relative safety of Great Britain. His forces were mauled at Dunkirk, but made it to England. At that moment in 1940, the Nazis appeared to be invincible. They had laid France low within weeks and had captured the Low Countries in days. They already had Austria, Norway, Czechoslovakia, and half of Poland. It seemed to the world as if England would fall like a ripe orange.

The French were broken in spirit. France, repository of the highest values in Western culture, lay broken and raped by the Hun. A somber mood of nighttime grimness leapt over France with extreme suddenness. In every city, there was terror and apprehension, from Lyons to Tours to Villefranche to Nancy to Paris, the City of Lights, itself.

It looked like France was finished, even to most Frenchmen.

In London, the emaciated General de Gaulle bent over his radio microphone at the BBC's European service. "Mes vieux," he said, "we face a period of protracted struggle," or similar words.

But exactly, General! That is exactly what everyone faces. Life is a period of protracted struggle. You have to understand that from the very outset. Then you have to try to understand it every day. At each and every triumph, at each and every trial, you have to remember that life is a protracted struggle. No two ways about it. For each and every person alive, there's a protracted struggle. No one gets a downhill ride all the way.

The nature of life as "struggle" is nowhere more clear than in the efforts of Bunkhouse Logicians to get their heart's desire, the goal that will make them proud of themselves. As the alert reader has noticed by now, the path is not for the fainthearted or the goldbricks.

It takes perseverance and lots of it to face the protracted struggle without resorting to false hopes and nostrums of the mind. To face life as it is through the powerful lens of the Bunkhouse Logician's eye is to see a difficult uphill battle to reach the promised land. There's rejection and humiliation and defeat before you realize that you've suddenly reached the sunny uplands of the human spirit.

How do you take the punishment of life without giving up? How do you get hit, let it bleed, then come back again to fight another day? Whence cometh the wellsprings of energy that are required?

First, there are the external magnets. There's the executive suite, pulling you toward it. There's the house on Nantucket, also pulling you in its direction. There's the leisure to live on Cape Hatteras and play whatever game is on your mind. There's a stack of Treasury bills up to your elbow telling you that you have financial security for the rest of your life. There's the applauding multitude as you receive your Nobel Prize. There's the throng of art critics clustered around you at that Manhattan gallery as your first show opens. There's the bevy of groupies wanting you to do anything—anything at all!—with them, just as long as you take note of their existence.

But even those powerful pulls on your psyche aren't enough to motivate you through difficult and painful hours. You must have not only that external pull, but also an internal push to get you where you want to go. Something irresistible inside you must propel you forward through all the mud and muck to the place where you want to be.

That something must be a feeling that you deserve the good things that are in your sights. The men and women who want to succeed and *will* succeed in this life will be those who believe that they *deserve* to succeed. The human spirit will not readily move to a place where it doesn't feel comfortable.

Be sure that if you do *not* feel as if you deserve to have that Bentley, you will not have it. If you feel as if you would *not* like to have lunch by Steven Spielberg's pool, you will never get there. If you feel as if you would be uncomfortable at the Detroit Economics Club, you will not find yourself there. If you would feel ill at ease at the Links Club, the problem is unlikely to arise, period.

One of the ineluctable signs of the great men and women of this world, those who wear their glories comfortably, who play the game to win, is that they *feel* worthy. They like themselves. Compare a Winston Churchill with a Jimmy Carter, or a de Gaulle with a John Major. In each case, the former wore their power gracefully because they were sure they deserved it. The latter always found power an ill-fitting garment because they never felt certain that they deserved it.

Bunkhouse Logic tells you that if you're to move up the one-way street of life to the off-ramp you want, you must have some affection for yourself. If you hate the person whose face appears in the mirror, how on earth can you make that person boldly ask for what he wants and get it? How do you get to like yourself? A great deal of liking yourself has to do with something simple and old-fashioned: *behaving* like a good person.

The more you behave in a way that lets you feel like a great human being, the more you're likely to *feel* like a great one. Similarly, the more you're likely to feel like you deserve the great things you want. If you believe, down in your heart, that you've acquitted yourself well in your contracts with your fellow human beings, you'll feel as if you deserve the good things that life can hold for you.

Bunkhouse Logic doesn't tell you to just behave shrewdly. Bunkhouse Logic tells you that you'll take off like a meteor when you behave both shrewdly *and* kindly. Yes, of course you mustn't forget that there are other people on this earth. If you begin to act as if you're the only person on this planet and as if it belonged to you for plunder and spoil, you're not going to like yourself very much. If, on the other hand, you take what you need, but don't steal or take from others who are in need, you'll admire yourself enough to move forward to your ultimate destination.

Yes, make the best deal you can when you get to the table. But if you trick the other players so that they suffer needlessly, you'll be far behind in the game. Eventually you'll completely lose the stomach for playing at all.

When you take your first steps up the rungs that lead to power and success, of course you should revel in your success. But don't take out your glee by kicking the fingers of those coming after you. If you do, you'll soon find that you've lost the confidence for the rest of the ascent.

Example: You're going great guns in your career as a real-estate salesman. You've stepped up to the table by asking to show only the most expensive co-ops on Manhattan's East Side. You've asked for what you want by telling your bosses that you want to be on straight commission instead of salary. You understand that life is as it is instead of how it should be by showing the house to 50 jerk-offs who didn't have the money to buy anyway.

Finally, you get a couple from Oklahoma who have just sold the farm. They're rolling in cash, and they don't know New York real estate from a hole in the ground. But Big Mama has always wanted to live in the Big Apple. You know that while the asking price of the co-op is $5 mil, it's not worth a dime over $3.5 million. But the folks from Oklahoma don't know that. The apartment is someone else's listing. Do you take the couple for all they're worth? Absolutely not. Instead, you give them advice about how to bid and how much. Pretty soon, they have the apartment at a fair price.

You've made a fine commission, and you can look yourself in the eye. You know that you're made of the stuff that will last and endure. You might have made a few thousand more, but you wouldn't be the kind of person you like. And that would have slowed you down in the long run.

Do It for Yourself

Joan D., one of the greatest geniuses of our time, once told me her beliefs about the universe. "I do not believe that there is a life after death," she said. "I wish I could, but I don't."

"What happens to you when you die?" I asked, because I believe her to be wise.

"What happens to a flower when it dies?" she answered.

"Then is there any reason to be good or generous or kind in this world?" I asked. "After all, there is, in your mind, no pain or reward in an afterlife."

Joan D. looked at me and said, "Yes, of course. You do those good things for yourself. That is all the reason you need. You do them so you'll feel good about yourself."

There may or may not be an afterlife. But Joan D. is absolutely correct when she promises that you'll feel better about yourself inasmuch as you treat people with respect and decency. That is its own reward. It warms your heart, and it makes you strong when you accomplish what you want to in this difficult world.

No precept of Bunkhouse Logic should come before acting in a way that will make you proud of yourself. Yes, you should avoid the company of unlucky people. But you must never act callous or cruel. The Sudanese people are unlucky, but Bunkhouse Logic would never tell you to ignore their misery. Even the sad people in your own life deserve your sympathy. You don't have to spend a lot of time with them, but neither should you act as if they're lepers. Act like a nice guy or girl. You'll feel proud and happy.

Yes, you should concentrate on how to and forget why not, but that doesn't call for a horrid ruthlessness that ignores the feelings of those around you. If you act ruthlessly with other people, you may be sure that you'll soon act ruthlessly toward yourself. Be kinder to people than they deserve and you'll reap the psychic and material benefits right here on earth.

One of the most interesting events in life is to attend meetings in law, in government, or in the entertainment business, where people are selected for hiring or promotion. To be on the inside and see what the criteria really are is no less than fascinating. Here, too, it's abundantly clear that nice guys finish first.

When men and women sit around long oak tables discussing whom to hire and promote, they always talk about their ability. They always talk about familiarity. But be assured on the honor of the bunkhouse that they also talk about who's a nice guy and who isn't.

"Hmm," says the chairman of the hiring committee, "X has a great head for figures."

"Hmm," adds the vice chairman, "he plays a mean hand of bridge over at the club, too."

"But you should hear him bawling out his assistant," objects the COO. "What a bastard."

"Hmm," says the chairman, fingering his silver Gucci pen, "let's forget about him."

"How about Y?" asks the vice chairman. "He's a smart fellow, too."

"Friendly around the bar as well," agrees the COO. "And you know that he spends a lot of time with his assistant's son. Poor kid's autistic."

"Hmm," says the COO. "I like that in a man."

You can bet that Y will get the job. And you can bet that Y is the person you want to be.

Those in a position to grant you your dreams and wishes—whether they be romantic, personal, occupational, creative, or in any area—will always prefer the more generous, kindly person over the less generous, less kindly person. Make sure you *are* that person. It will make you feel good. Others will notice it and will prefer you for it.

Think of the cowboy. He hangs out at the bunkhouse all the livelong day. He deals with the same folks day in and day out. There's Cookie, the cook. Then there's Lucky, the trail boss; Butch, the ace wrangler; and Skip, the water boy. As the life of the cowboy progresses, he knows very well indeed that he has to be nice to the people he deals with. He may be one up on one or more of them from time to time, but that won't make him act cruelly. He knows that the same people will eventually have the opportunity to judge *him.* They'll be looking to see if he acts generously when he's up, just so they'll know how to treat him when he's down.

That cowboy, the paragon of the bunkhouse, knows full well that if he acts like a nice guy to everyone else, he'll come out miles ahead when they're judging *him.* He uses his inner mobility to be kind, his activity to be generous to others. They won't feel as if he's the kind of bushwhacker who might ambush them when they feel low. And they'll feel that they can trust him no matter what.

But more than that, the cowboy knows something else. On those incredibly lonely nights when he wonders how he goes on, he has high opinions of himself, by himself, to fall back on. He knows that when he wonders why he lives and others die, he'll have warm feelings about himself to keep himself going. He'll have enough pride in the ways he's acted toward others to keep himself moving in life's often painful journey down that one-way street.

So should it be with suburban and urban cowboys. You may not be out on the prairie alone. But you *are* alone. And to make it through life's travails, to continue to play the game with pride and energy—the only winning way—you need to feel good about yourself. To climb up toward that magnificent summit of hopes and joys where your heart's desire lies, you must have self-worth above all else. You must allow others to think highly of you and choose you, and you must love yourself enough to persevere.

Nice guys finish first. Be one and win.

CONCLUSION

Learning the rules of Bunkhouse Logic is the easy part. Living them is the part that takes strength and patience. It's also the part that brings you the accomplishments you've always wanted, the ones you've always dreamed of. Bunkhouse Logic swears to you that if you can put these precepts into practice over time, you'll see your fantasies turn into reality.

If you live by the rules of the bunkhouse, there's only one more danger: not thinking big enough. Think your biggest thoughts. Dream your biggest dreams. The logic of the bunkhouse, in theory and in practice, will make them real.

Through that accomplishment will come a full heart. Through those achievements will come the pride in yourself that makes a fulfilled life. Through getting what you want from life will come the feeling of contentment that you have always longed for.

By employing the logic of the bunkhouse, you will bring into your life the achievement that's the food of happiness you've been hungering for. The time to start is now.

ABOUT THE AUTHOR

Ben Stein can be seen talking about finance on Fox TV news every week and writing about it regularly in *The New York Times* Sunday Business section. No wonder: Not only is he the son of the world-famous economist and government adviser Herbert Stein, but Ben is a respected economist in his own right. He received his B.A. with honors in economics from Columbia University in 1966, studied economics in the graduate school of economics at Yale while he earned his law degree there, and worked as an economist for the Department of Commerce.

Ben Stein is known to many as a movie and television personality, especially from *Ferris Bueller's Day Off* and from his long-running quiz show, *Win Ben Stein's Money*. But he has probably worked more in personal and corporate finance than anything else. He has written about finance for *Barron's* and *The Wall Street Journal* for decades. He was one of the chief busters of the junk-bond frauds of the 1980s, has been a long-time critic of corporate executives' self-dealing, and has written three self-help books about personal finance. He frequently travels the country speaking about finance in both serious and humorous ways, and is a regular contributor to the CBS Sunday Morning News.

Website: **www.benstein.com**

Hay House Titles of Related Interest

Empowerment Cards for Inspired Living, by Tavis Smiley

Everyday Positive Thinking, by Louise L. Hay and Friends

Passionate People Produce:
Rekindle Your Passion and Creativity—
A Blueprint for Business People, by Charles Kovess

10 Secrets for Success and Inner Peace,
by Dr. Wayne W. Dyer

Who Are You? A Success Process for Building Your Life's Foundation,
by Stedman Graham

You Can Have an Amazing Life . . . in Just 60 Days!
by Dr. John F. Demartini

※ ※ ※

All of the above are available at your local bookstore,
or may be ordered through Hay House (see next page).

※ ※ ※

We hope you enjoyed this Hay House book.If you'd like to receive a free catalog featuring additional Hay House books and products, or if you'd like information about the Hay Foundation, please contact:

Hay House, Inc.
P.O. Box 5100
Carlsbad, CA 92018-5100

(760) 431-7695 or **(800) 654-5126**
(760) 431-6948 (fax) or **(800) 650-5115 (fax)**
www.hayhouse.com® • **www.hayfoundation.org**

※ ※ ※

Published and distributed in Australia by:
Hay House Australia Pty. Ltd. • 18/36 Ralph St. • Alexandria NSW 2015
Phone: 612-9669-4299 • *Fax:* 612-9669-4144 • www.hayhouse.com.au

Published and distributed in the United Kingdom by:
Hay House UK, Ltd. • Unit 62, Canalot Studios • 222 Kensal Rd., London
W10 5BN • *Phone:* 44-20-8962-1230 • *Fax:* 44-20-8962-1239
www.hayhouse.co.uk

Published and distributed in the Republic of South Africa by:
Hay House SA (Pty), Ltd., P.O. Box 990, Witkoppen 2068
Phone/Fax: 27-11-706-6612 • orders@psdprom.co.za

Published in India by:
Hay House Publications (India) Pvt. Ltd., 3 Hampton Court, A-Wing,
123 Wodehouse Rd., Colaba, Mumbai 400005 • *Phone:* 91 (22)
22150557 or 22180533 • *Fax:* 91 (22) 22839619
www.hayhouseindia.co.in

Distributed in India by:
Media Star, 7 Vaswani Mansion, 120 Dinshaw Vachha Rd., Churchgate,
Mumbai 400020 • *Phone:* 91 (22) 22815538-39-40
Fax: 91 (22) 22839619 • booksdivision@mediastar.co.in

Distributed in Canada by:
Raincoast • 9050 Shaughnessy St.,
Vancouver, B.C. V6P 6E5 • *Phone:* (604) 323-7100 • *Fax:* (604) 323-2600

※ ※ ※

Tune in to **HayHouseRadio.com**™ for the best in inspirational talk radio featuring top Hay House authors! And, sign up via the Hay House USA Website to receive the Hay House online newsletter and stay informed about what's going on with your favorite authors. You'll receive bimonthly announcements about: Discounts and Offers, Special Events, Product Highlights, Free Excerpts, Giveaways, and more!
www.hayhouse.com®